Teaching Physical Education to Children with Autism

This book is an essential guide for how to teach fun and engaging physical education classes tailored to include the needs of autistic children and children with learning disabilities.

With this practical guidebook detailing tested methods and best practices, teachers will be well equipped to support all students, including disabled students and those with varying support needs. Through a narrative lens that details children's real-life journeys, and with key definitions and ready-to-use activities included throughout, *Teaching Physical Education to Children with Autism* presents a teacher's first-hand account of what it's like to teach students with diverse learning needs. Its comprehensive scope addresses all the practical challenges that educators may face in working with this population, including difficult behavior and disengagement.

Detailing a myriad of solutions to try, along with flexible frameworks that can be applied to a myriad of physical education goals, this book is essential reading for any physical education teacher, special education teacher, and anyone wishing to create more equitable learning environments for children with varying learning needs.

Bill Mokin has been a teacher for 35 years and worked with students of all ages from pre-school to adult. He has taught physical education to students with disabilities/special needs for 16 years and has been recognized as the special education/inclusion authority by the the elementary physical education team in the Issaquah School District in Washington, US.

Also Available from Routledge Eye On Education
(www.routledge.com/k-12)

Shaking Up Special Education: Instructional Moves to Increase Achievement
Savanna Flakes

Specially Designed Instruction: Increasing Success for Students with Disabilities
Anne M. Beninghof

The Complete Guide to Special Education: Expert Advice on Evaluations, IEPs, and Helping Kids Succeed
Linda Wilmshurst and Alan W. Brue

Loving Your Job in Special Education: 50 Tips and Tools
Rachel R. Jorgensen

Learning Through Movement in the K-6 Classroom: Integrating Theater and Dance to Achieve Educational Equity
Kelly Mancini Becker

Lesson Plans for the Elementary PE Teacher: A Developmental Movement Education & Skill-Themes Framework
Michael Gosset

Teaching Physical Education to Children with Autism: Stories from the Field
Bill Mokin

Teaching Physical Education to Children with Autism
Stories from the Field

Bill Mokin

Taylor & Francis Group
NEW YORK AND LONDON

Designed cover image: © Bill Mokin

First published 2024
by Routledge
605 Third Avenue, New York, NY 10158

and by Routledge
4 Park Square, Milton Park, Abingdon, Oxon, OX14 4RN

Routledge is an imprint of the Taylor & Francis Group, an informa business

© 2024 Bill Mokin

The right of Bill Mokin to be identified as author of this work has been asserted in accordance with sections 77 and 78 of the Copyright, Designs and Patents Act 1988.

All rights reserved. No part of this book may be reprinted or reproduced or utilised in any form or by any electronic, mechanical, or other means, now known or hereafter invented, including photocopying and recording, or in any information storage or retrieval system, without permission in writing from the publishers.

Trademark notice: Product or corporate names may be trademarks or registered trademarks, and are used only for identification and explanation without intent to infringe.

ISBN: 978-1-032-57122-5 (hbk)
ISBN: 978-1-032-56901-7 (pbk)
ISBN: 978-1-003-43790-1 (ebk)

DOI: 10.4324/9781003437901

Typeset in Palatino
by SPi Technologies India Pvt Ltd (Straive)

To my beloved wife, Dona

Contents

Acknowledgments xi

Introduction – 3 Building Blocks 1
   The First Building Block – Trust Yourself 1
   The Second Building Block – Why Am I Here? 2
   The Third Building Block – Joy! 3
   Becoming an Educator 4

1 Definitions and Essential Concepts 7
   Physical Education, Autism, Special Education,
   Free Appropriate Public Education (FAPE), Individuals
   with Disabilities Education Act (IDEA), Least Restrictive
   Environment (LRE), Mainstreaming, Inclusion,
   Certificated & Classified Employee, Paraeducator 7
   Think about It Questions 17

2 Elements of Effective Instruction 19
   The Importance of an Inventor Mindset 19
   Individualized Education Program (IEP), Lesson
   Plans that Fit Your Students 21
   Paraeducators Are an Integral Part of the Team 26
   One-to-One Instruction 28
   Learning Prompts 29
   The Power of Voice 30
   Music 32
   Your Own Inner Resources 34
   What Does Inclusion Look Like? 36
   Being the Teacher of Record 41
   Think about It Questions 42

3 Organization, Systems, and Routine 44
Anchor Charts 44
Getting Prepared: Warmup, Home Base,
Grouping Strategies 46
Routines and Scaffolds Benefit Diverse Learners 48
The Track: A Mobile Learning Platform 52
Station Rotations 53
Think about It Questions 54

4 Understanding Behavior, Sensory Diversity, and Challenges to Engagement 56
Connecting with Students Who Have Special Needs 57
Behavior Is Communication 59
Behavior Triggers (The World of Unexpected Things) 61
Hiking and Eloping 65
Two Helpful Tools: Functional Behavior Assessment &
Behavior Intervention Plan 67
Repetitive Movements and Vocalizations 69
Protecting a Student's Dignity and Modesty 70
Managing the Rest of the Class When One
Student Escalates 72
Maintaining Student Engagement 74
Sensory Diversity 76
What Does It Mean to "Pay Attention," and
Why Is It so Complicated? 79
Staying Focused When There Are so Many
Distractions: Ramp up Your Learning Prompts 83
Positive Behavior Support 86
Think about It Questions 88

5 Incremental Steps to Learning 91
Authenticity, Dependability and Trust 91
Consistent Routine: The Warmup 92
Direct Instruction: The Learning Circle 95
Communication Clarity and Total Physical
Response 97
I Learn a Lesson and a Different Way
to Communicate 102

Eye Contact: Toss and Catch, Moving to the Ball 104
Small Motor Activities to Practice Visual Attention:
Stack Cups 106
Lesson Plans: Body Awareness and Balance 108
Functional and Socializing Skills, Outdoor
Play Structures 111
Think about It Questions 114

6 Fitness Activities for Better Health 116

Fitness Components 117
Flexibility and Locomotor Activities 120
Lesson Plans: Body Composition and Nutrition 123
Cardiorespiratory Endurance, Running,
and Other Options 130
Muscle Strengthening Activities and
Physical Prompts 135
Think about It Questions 140

7 From Non-Locomotor to Locomotor 141

Transition from the Learning Circle to the Track 141
The Mat Circle: Locomotor 143
Stepping with Modifications 146
Wheels 149
Ball Striking 151
Bowling 155
Build Learning in Stages: Toss and Catch,
Climbing Wall 157
Lesson Plans: Upgrade the Track with Variations 159
Mat Work and Challenge Courses 162
Think about It Questions 166

8 Proactive Strategies for Staying on Task 168

Playing a Game, and What Happens When
It Falls Apart 168
Prerequisite Game Skills 172
Engineer the Space 173
Use More Staff or Helping Buddies 176

Reduce the Distance between Players; Bring
　　　Play Closer to the Ground 177
　　　Create New Roles 178
　　　Break the Lesson Down into Pieces 179
　　　Think about It Questions 180

9　Curriculum, Lesson Design, Scope, and Sequence 182
　　　Interplay between Standards, Units, and
　　　SMART Goals: Jump Rope and Challenge Course 182
　　　Assessment & Measuring Growth 190
　　　Think about It Questions 194

10　Collaborating to Meet Challenges. 196
　　　Being a Special Educator 196
　　　Parents, Students, and Teachers: A Partnership 201
　　　Window or Iceberg? Shared Insights 204
　　　Think about It Questions 205

11　Looking Forward. 207
　　　Start with the Child 207
　　　Successes and Failures 209
　　　What More Can We do? 211
　　　Teachers Are Diverse Learners and Sensory
　　　Processors Too 213
　　　Some Thoughts about Uncovering the Inventor
　　　in Each of Us 214
　　　Think about It Questions 215

Epilogue 217

References. 221
Index 223

Acknowledgments

I would like to thank all my students. They trusted me and they allowed me to lead them. They were also the means by which I could find fulfillment and joy as a teacher. Second, I thank all my educator colleagues who were my second family for so many years and who shared so much. I want to acknowledge the specific contributions of four of them. First, my longtime friend Sara Jo Pietraszewski, who was the first colleague to read the manuscript. Her enthusiasm, integrity, and insight have added much to this book, as they have enriched our friendship. Second, Jaime Mallamo, a wonderful, dedicated special educator. I will always cherish the hours we spent in lawn chairs in the school parking lot during the scary first summer of the Covid pandemic combing through the chapters so I would avoid errors and flawed concepts. Those work meetings provided the basis for many of the improvements we made to our PE program the following school year. I must acknowledge the debt I owe to Martin Block, author and Professor in the School of Education and Human Development, University of Virginia, who amazed me with his encouragement and generosity, reading several chapters and guiding me through my very first publication – a portion of the manuscript that he helped edit and make suitable for inclusion in *Palaestra*, the journal for Adapted Sport, Physical Education, and Recreational Therapy. I have cited his work numerous times. Helping angels come from unexpected places. I first encountered Michelle Grenier, author and Professor Emeritus at the University of New Hampshire, and past president of NCPEID (National Consortium of Physical Education for Individuals with Disabilities) in a "What's New in Adapted Physical Education" podcast. Her emphasis on the importance of "regular" PE teachers and the need for more training and collaboration obviously struck me. Without hesitating, she agreed to correspond when

I reached out. Our subsequent emails, texts, and phone conversations helped reassure me that I was on the right track.

Finally, my late wife, Dona, was the first to read the manuscript, and she was an unflinchingly sharp editor. When I took the lazy way out and described people or events with generalizations or clichés, she called it out and forced me to spell out exactly what I meant.

Introduction

3 Building Blocks

My summer as a counselor at Camp R in upstate New York set in place the very first formal building blocks for becoming a teacher. These were things I learned and ritualized and recall today when I teach.

The First Building Block – Trust Yourself

This was the concept that I could help my campers by trusting my own judgment and being authentic. While that was something they told us prior to campers arriving, the truth of it was born out time and time again over the next two months. It's a simple concept but not always simple to do. Your willingness to be yourself communicates your trust in others and invites their trust in return. In being authentic, you are communicating dependability and predictability. That is a strong basis for living and learning together. Summer camp is the ideal environment for enabling this. Games, nature, friends, and new discoveries are everywhere. Everything around us is conducive to having fun together, but we also eat and sleep together. Not only do we share our living space, but we also share our stories. We each come with our own background and habits, and when we share this much intimacy, we can't help just being who we are. At the end of the summer, you go home a changed person. You've grown in every possible way, and it is due to the independence you've achieved away from home, the relationships you've formed, and the new experiences you have shared. It all builds confidence and maturity.

What did it mean as a nineteen-year-old to "trust" my campers? Right off the bat, many of the counselors had to confront a certain amount of unfamiliarity, discomfort, and even fear relating to our situation. For some of us, this was our first real job. Many had never been this far from home. Most had never had this kind of responsibility entrusted to them. We understood that many of our campers would have disabilities, illness, and special needs. There were a lot of unknowns. One could accept that fact, open one's mind and heart, and jump in with both feet. Or perhaps step in carefully. Either way, we had to have some trust and some faith that we would be okay, that we would figure it out, that we wouldn't screw up too badly. How hard could it be to *just be yourself?*

The Second Building Block – Why Am I Here?

This one is so essential that I would refer to it as the "cornerstone." It is to remember why you're there. The answer: to serve the interests of the kids. That your own interests are served in the process is a corollary benefit. If you can just remember that you are there and getting paid to put the kids' interests first, you are not likely to get into trouble with authorities. On the first day of class one of my professors in the teaching program at Sonoma State remarked (with only half a smile) that our most important job as a first-year teacher was to not get fired! Laughs all around. However, the subtext to that remark was a warning not to do anything really stupid – basically, to remember *why* you're standing in a classroom in front of a bunch of kids.

Why do people become so passionate about working with students who have special needs? It could be hard to understand if you have not had the experience. The best way I can explain it is that the biggest joy of teaching is connecting with your students, and this happens in the emotional arena as well as the academic arena. It is quantitatively and qualitatively harder to make these kinds of connections with my students who have certain disabilities. The successes can be the product of so much hard work that when they occur; it is a delight to the soul. It is also clear how much my students rely on me for support and guidance, and therefore it is not difficult to keep their interests front and center. There were eight boys in my cabin at Camp R who relied on me, and it was a fulltime 24 hour-a-day job. To learn that lesson at the age of nineteen was one of the great gifts I received that summer.

The Third Building Block – Joy!

This is the helium block. Maybe it helps to lighten the "heaviness" of the other two: You should be enjoying yourself. Every teacher goes through periods of despondency, and there are so many things to get potentially despondent over: unreachable students, lack of resources, being weighed down under an avalanche of initiatives and regulations, the unceasing incoming tide of ideas you've seen before that are masquerading as "new" and "great" accompanied by a never-ending parade of new slogans and jargon in which we are mercilessly churned. Sometimes it's difficult to come up for air, and you want to scream, "Please leave me alone for a month with nothing new to think about so I can just focus on what I love to do: teach my kids!"

If you're not enjoying your job, change your methods. Experiment. Be open to advice from trusted colleagues. Take a few personal days to reflect. Listen to your heart when you wake up with that feeling of dread about the upcoming day and the lesson plan that may not reflect your best work and scrap it. Declare it **Free Choice Day.** If you are a classroom teacher, put together a bunch of art supplies in different media, some wood scraps, old Tinker Toys and glue, and tell your students that they are going to create something out of all these components. The truly valuable part of the day may not be what they end up building or painting, but the amazing conversations you have with them during those relaxing yet creative hours. I have done this several times in my career, and the feeling tone of the class after a Free Choice Day is much lighter than it was before.

My PE version of Free Choice Day is similar. I put out a bunch of carefully selected equipment with consideration to the behavior its use is likely to cause, and I remind them it's not recess. PE safety and respect rules still apply. It is also essential to explain why the class is getting a Free Choice Day. It may be a pre-planned reward. Or it may be an opportunity for them to show me how maturely they can play together. That may be the single goal I set. A more structured version of Free Choice Day is **Invent-a-Game Day**. I run this as a station rotation and give a lot of thought to the collection of materials and equipment I place at each station. The explicit goals are for teams to 1. examine what they find at the station 2. discuss 3. invent a game out of the materials 4. cooperate. My assessment tool when I visit a team is selecting someone at random to explain the rules of their game.

Becoming an Educator

Before becoming a physical educator, I spent the first half of my career as an English as a Second Language specialist. I was a teacher and program director. My postgraduate work was in linguistics and language acquisition. This turned out to be very useful preparation for working with students whose biggest challenge was often language and communication. In 2006, I had the opportunity to switch fields to physical education. As a PE teacher, I have always had classes of students with special needs as well as classes of students who were neurotypical.[1] Of the students who qualified for special education services, most have had Autism Spectrum Disorder (ASD). Doctors and therapists know more about autism and the various other disabilities and diagnoses of the children that I teach than I do. My job has never been to cure or provide therapy. It is to provide an appropriate physical education program for all students, regardless of disability or other impactful condition. I have learned to do that from many years of experience.

In the winter of 2019–2020 the students with special needs at our school were very much on my mind. I had written a grant for a large quantity of gymnastics mats and specialized equipment to provide a richer and more suitable environment for my students with disabilities. In the process of writing the grant application I had to answer a lot of questions. Why did I think this equipment was necessary? How did I plan to use it? How would I know if the students benefited from it? Could it be used with all students in an inclusive general education PE class, and what would that look like? I could not answer those questions without thinking about my students – about specific students. That formed much of the content of the journal I began during the coronavirus remote teaching time in 2020. It felt natural to write about certain students who had made a significant impact on me. They came as a smaller group to a PE class that I designed to meet their specific needs. There were two such classes: one for students in kindergarten, first and second grade and another for students in third, fourth and fifth. The students I had in mind were children who not only made a lasting impression on me, but who also presented distinctly different instructional challenges. These challenges, in turn, caused me to embark on new and different adventures in teaching. As I started to write about each of them, I continually found myself reflecting on how each of these students made me grow as a teacher.

In the following pages, I present methods, advice, and opinions about teaching in a public school environment, and these are backed up by teaching experience and by what I have learned from the wonderful people with whom I have worked. Collaborating with other professionals and with the people who know my students best is essential to being well informed. Usually, the information teachers need is not handed to us, and we must search for it. Our district's autism and behavior specialists present trainings every year or two for our staff. The trainings are helpful but rarely address physical education. It has always been up to individual teachers to seek out collaboration with those people who can provide the help they need. We have a huge amount of combined knowledge and expertise among our colleagues. The special education teachers, counselors, psychologists, occupational therapists (OTs), physical therapists (PTs) and speech language pathologists (SLPs) who we have on staff at every school building are our first go-to source since they are nearby. Of the thirty elementary PE teachers in our district, four of us teach classes designed for students who have special needs, and we meet once a month. Based on the belief that the most useful kind of professional development is to observe a good teacher teach (though these tend to be rare opportunities), the approach of this book is to give the reader the experience of being in the gym and on the playing field with real students, teachers and paraeducators. The fact that all names, physical descriptions, and many identifying features have been changed to protect privacy does not detract from the truthfulness of the information.

In writing this book, I have always kept my teaching colleagues in mind and tried to anticipate the kinds of questions they would have. I am confident that PE teachers will relate to these stories, and that anyone who teaches diverse learners or has a personal relationship to children with special needs will too. The world of disabilities and special education is foreign to most people, teachers included, unless they have had personal experience. Ignorance leads to doubt, hesitancy, and lack of confidence, particularly because we are aware that there is a history of injustice surrounding minority populations, and the last thing we want is to perpetuate inequities and stereotypes. For that reason, some may find that approaching this subject and these students through the eyes of a PE teacher and not a clinician or academic is an appealing way to approach the subject. The narrative portions of this book allow the reader to get to know some of my students, and I hope that their stories enliven these pages.

Note

1 Special educators sometimes refer to the General Education student population as "neurotypical," or they might say that students with disabilities must be educated with students who are "neurotypical."

1
Definitions and Essential Concepts

Physical Education, Autism, Special Education, Free Appropriate Public Education (FAPE), Individuals with Disabilities Education Act (IDEA), Least Restrictive Environment (LRE), Mainstreaming, Inclusion, Certificated & Classified Employee, Paraeducator

> "The goal of physical education is to develop physically literate individuals who have the knowledge, skills and confidence to enjoy a lifetime of healthful physical activity."
>
> (*National Standards & Grade-Level Outcomes for K-12 Physical Education*, Society of Health and Physical Educators, SHAPE)

In Washington state where I work, the Office of Superintendent of Public Instruction has established K-12 Learning Standards and assessments in all subject areas, including physical education and has adopted SHAPE's National K-12 Standards almost verbatim. These standards define in broad terms what PE teachers are responsible for teaching. These are the **Physical Education K-12 Learning Standards**:

- Standard 1: Students will demonstrate competency in a variety of motor skills and movement patterns.
- Standard 2: Students will apply knowledge of concepts, principles, strategies, and tactics related to movement and performance.
- Standard 3: Students will demonstrate the knowledge and skills to achieve and maintain a health-enhancing level of physical activity and fitness.
- Standard 4: Students will exhibit responsible personal and social behavior that respects self and others.
- Standard 5: Students will recognize the value of physical activity for health, enjoyment, challenge, self-expression, and social interaction.

Autism Spectrum Disorder (ASD), as defined by the Individuals with Disabilities Education Act (IDEA), is "a developmental disability significantly affecting verbal and nonverbal communication and social interaction, generally evident before the age of three, that adversely affects a child's educational performance" (U.S. Department of Education, https://sites.ed.gov/idea/).

The American Psychiatric Association's Diagnostic and Statistical Manual, Fifth Edition (DSM-5) provides standardized criteria to help diagnose Autism Spectrum Disorder (ASD). To meet diagnostic criteria for ASD according to DSM-5, a child must have persistent deficits in *each* of three areas of social communication and interaction (see **A.1.** through **A.3.** below) plus *at least two of four* types of restricted, repetitive behaviors (see **B.1.** through **B.4.** below).

   A. Persistent deficits in social communication and social interaction across multiple contexts, as manifested by the following, currently or by history (examples are illustrative, not exhaustive):
      1. Deficits in social-emotional reciprocity, ranging, for example, from abnormal social approach and failure of normal back-and-forth conversation; to reduced

sharing of interests, emotions, or affect; to failure to initiate or respond to social interactions.
2. Deficits in nonverbal communicative behaviors used for social interaction, ranging, for example, from poorly integrated verbal and nonverbal communication; to abnormalities in eye contact and body language or deficits in understanding and use of gestures; to a total lack of facial expressions and nonverbal communication.
3. Deficits in developing, maintaining, and understanding relationships, ranging, for example, from difficulties adjusting behavior to suit various social contexts; to difficulties in sharing imaginative play or in making friends; to absence of interest in peers.

B. Restricted, repetitive patterns of behavior, interests, or activities, as manifested by at least two of the following, currently or by history (examples are illustrative, not exhaustive):
1. Stereotyped or repetitive motor movements, use of objects, or speech (e.g., simple motor stereotypes, lining up toys or flipping objects, echolalia, idiosyncratic phrases).
2. Insistence on sameness, inflexible adherence to routines, or ritualized patterns of verbal or nonverbal behavior (e.g., extreme distress at small changes, difficulties with transitions, rigid thinking patterns, greeting rituals, need to take same route or eat same food every day).
3. Highly restricted, fixated interests that are abnormal in intensity or focus (e.g., strong attachment to or preoccupation with unusual objects, excessively circumscribed or perseverative interests).
4. Hyper- or hyporeactivity to sensory input or unusual interest in sensory aspects of the environment (e.g. apparent indifference to pain/temperature, adverse response to specific sounds or textures, excessive smelling or touching of objects, visual fascination with lights or movement).

C. Symptoms must be present in the early developmental period (but may not become fully manifest until social demands exceed limited capacities, or may be masked by learned strategies in later life).
D. Symptoms cause clinically significant impairment in social, occupational, or other important areas of current functioning.
E. These disturbances are not better explained by intellectual disability (intellectual developmental disorder) or global developmental delay. Intellectual disability and autism spectrum disorder frequently co-occur; to make comorbid diagnoses of autism spectrum disorder and intellectual disability, social communication should be below that expected for general developmental level.

As startling as the CDC's latest estimate on the prevalence of autism is, I find the steady bi-annual increase in incidence to be even more so.

DSM 5's definition of ASD matches closely with my own experience of a significant percentage of my students who

Surveillance Year	Birth Year	About 1 in X Children
2020	2012	1 in 36
2018	2010	1 in 44
2016	2008	1 in 54
2014	2006	1 in 59
2012	2004	1 in 69
2010	2002	1 in 68
2008	2000	1 in 88
2006	1998	1 in 110
2004	1996	1 in 125
2002	1994	1 in 150

FIGURE 1.1 Identified Prevalence of Autism Spectrum Disorder among Children Aged 3–17 Years. Centers for Disease Control and Prevention, https://www.cdc.gov/ncbddd/autism/data.html

have qualified for special education services. Deficits in *social-emotional reciprocity* that I often see are failure to initiate and have back and forth conversation, and difficulty being spontaneous in sharing enjoyment or interests with others. Lack of facial expression, eye contact, and non-verbal behaviors used for social interaction are also familiar traits among my students as are difficulty understanding social relationships and adjusting behavior in different social situations. Features of *atypical social communication* that I often see are the tendency to focus attention on only one topic and echolalia (repeating or echoing other people's language). *Atypical social development* manifests as a lack of peer relationships, and I have found that this is a particular concern to parents. Hand and finger mannerisms and motor patterns are common *repetitive behaviors*. I would also include reliance on certain toys, objects, or fidgets. Occasional self-harm and aggression are examples of *problem behavior*, but elopement or fleeing the instructional area is more common. *Sensory disorders* can take some time to identify. A student may appear agitated or confused, and the cause could be a sensory issue that the student is unable to articulate, such as a smell, noise, lighting, sudden movements, or bouncing balls.

When we talk about people who have severely impactful physical or cognitive conditions, it is good to remember that those conditions do not define them. They are people with their own traits and individuality who happen to have a diagnosis. The way they appear to others is a product not of their diagnosis but, in part, of their responses to their diagnosis. What we see when we look at our family members or our students or friends who have ASD is not the diagnosis, but a person who is learning to navigate the world with a collection of attributes of their diagnosis, and no two persons' journeys are exactly alike. I don't know if it's even that helpful to fix on a specific definition of autism. When I look at my students, I don't see a diagnosis. I see a young person trying to emerge, an individual with inner strengths and resources finding their way. I see it as my job to discover how I can help them in their journey. One of the hallmarks of teaching minority populations like students with special needs and English Language Learners is that we constantly strive to keep these students from being sidelined out of the mainstream. We work with them to overcome the gaps they are trying to cross to become an equal and a confident member of the learning community.

Students who have distinct learning needs, who have been tested according to state and local guidelines with the permission of their parents, may qualify for **special education** services. This is a term we will use frequently. Washington State defines special education as follows:

> Special education is specially designed instruction that addresses the unique needs of a student eligible to receive special education services. Special education is provided at no cost to parents and includes the related services a student needs to access her/his educational program."
> (Washington Office of Superintendent of Public Instruction (OSPI))

Special Education services are based on two federal laws.

> School Age (ages 3–21) students with disabilities who are determined eligible for special education and related services are entitled to a **Free Appropriate Public Education (FAPE)**. Services are provided to eligible students according to an Individualized Education Program (IEP) in preschools, elementary, and secondary schools, or other appropriate settings. The **Individuals with Disabilities Education Act (IDEA)** is the federal law that guarantees FAPE is provided to eligible students with disabilities. The Washington state regulations on special education can be found in the Washington Administrative Code (WAC) Chapter 392-172A.[1]

Just as the names for different racial and ethnic groups continually change over the years to reflect our culture, the labels given to people who have conditions that society says put them outside of "typical" range have also changed. When I started teaching, it was acceptable to refer to students with ASD, intellectual delays, and other types of impactful conditions as "special education students" or "special ed. students" or in written form, "SPED students." I no longer see those terms used in that way. Now, it is acceptable practice to identify students as "having special needs" or "with special needs." The distinction is that the condition does not define the person. It is an aspect of the person. People who work in the field of special education frequently remind us to use "person-first" language, as in "the young man with the hearing impairment," or "William has been diagnosed with Autism Spectrum Disorder." That is an easy way to remember the convention. It makes a lot of sense to me, however, the pendulum has begun to swing the other way, and there is a trend back to using "autistic" as an adjective. My advice: if unsure, ask. Being open and admitting uncertainty is a lot better than offending people.

One thing that has remained while the names have changed is that for decades public schools have been providing services for students who require them so that they can access an educational program. Special Education is a continuum of service options. All students are **General Education**[2] (gen. ed.) students first. Additional services are added for them to benefit from the public education to which they are entitled. This concept of "entitlement" is codified in U.S. law. **FAPE** is a cornerstone of U.S. education law under Section 504 of the Rehabilitation Act of 1973 that requires all schools that receive federal funding "…to provide a 'free appropriate public education' (FAPE) to each qualified person with a disability who is in the school district's jurisdiction, regardless of the nature or severity of the person's disability." The law defines various forms that "appropriate education" can take, including "…education in regular classes, education in regular classes with the use of related aids and services, or special education and related services in separate classrooms for all or portions of the school day…"[3]

In the district where I now teach, students who are tested and qualify for more moderate special education services are placed in Learning Resource Center – LRC I. Students with more extensive needs qualify for LRC II. LRC I students visit another classroom for about 30 minutes a day to receive help in the academic areas where they need it as determined by their Individualized Education Program (IEP). LRC II students spend a portion of their school day in a class designed to provide them with an appropriate educational program. They join their gen. ed. peers for certain subjects as stipulated by their IEP. Regarding physical education and special services, the IDEA law, **Sec. 300.108 Physical Education**, states:

> The State must ensure that public agencies in the State comply with the following:
>
> a. General, Physical education services, specially designed, if necessary, must be made available to every child with a disability receiving FAPE, unless the public agency enrolls children without disabilities and does not provide physical education to children without disabilities in the same grades.
> b. Regular physical education. Each child with a disability must be afforded the opportunity to participate in the regular physical education program available to nondisabled children unless –
>   1. The child is enrolled full time in a separate facility; or
>   2. The child needs specially designed physical education, as prescribed in the child's IEP.
> c. Special physical education. If specially designed physical education is prescribed in a child's IEP, the public agency responsible for the education of that child must provide the services directly or make arrangements for those services to be provided through other public or private programs.

According to the Center for Parent Information & Resources, a central hub of information and products created for families of children with disabilities, "**LRE** (Least Restrictive Environment) refers to the setting where a child with a disability can receive an appropriate education designed to meet his or her educational needs, alongside peers without disabilities to the maximum extent appropriate." LRE provisions are found within IDEA law. Adhering to the principle of Least Restrictive Environment, it is the IEP team that determines the actual placement of a student within a continuum of options: in regular classes, special classes, special schools, home instruction or instruction in hospitals and institutions. In my district's IEP forms, under Educational Services and Placement, the IEP team must answer the question, "Will the student participate in regular physical education? Yes/No." If "No" is checked, then the team defines the placement. For those students in my specially designed/modified PE class, their IEPs state: "_____ will participate in a modified PE class with other peers in LRC2 led by a general education PE teacher."

Because no one label or diagnosis fits all these students, and because it is cumbersome to continue referring to this group of students as "my special education students" or "my class of students with special needs," I looked for a way to refer to them throughout the book that was more streamlined. All the classrooms in our building have a plaque outside the door with the teacher's name and room number. Teachers commonly tack on some friendly text and photos to make the entrance more welcoming. Many teachers post one of their baby pictures. Others have posted a team name for their class that the students have voted on, such as "Ms. Granger's Gang." Outside of room 407, the plaque reads: "LRC II. Room 407. Finley's Fireflies." I've noticed that the name changes throughout the year. At one point frogs were involved. When I refer to my students who spend most of their day in the LRC II classroom, I will refer to them as my room 407 class or my Fireflies. It is partly out of expedience and partly to avoid falling into the outmoded label trap.

It is a good idea to read the state and federal laws that apply to your students. The law regarding **Least Restrictive Environment** is based on the idea that segregation of students should be avoided, and inclusion is desirable: But more importantly, over time you will develop a kind of "conscience" or compulsion that all of us who teach special populations acquire. It is always in the back of your mind, reminding you that your students who have limited English, have ASD, developmental delays, physical disabilities and who may be nonverbal are equal members of the school family and must participate in a meaningful way with everyone else. If you add together all of these "minority" groups of students and combine them with those additional students we've all encountered who don't self-advocate or call attention to themselves but seem to slip under the radar and evoke a nagging sense that they need our attention, this minority may in fact approach a majority of the students that we teach!

"**Mainstreaming**," and now "**inclusion**," have been the terms used to describe the process of placing students with disabilities in classes with students without disabilities and with the appropriate supports as determined by their IEP (Block 2016, pp. 23–24). As a teacher, how do I view my role in that process? Viewing every class and lesson as a further step along the "onramp"[4] helps me to put what I do in perspective. The "main stream" is always in sight, just slightly uphill from us. That means I always want my students to be on the onramp leading to the general education environment. I want them to be able to join their classmates who do not have disabilities in PE as soon as possible – just like they do at recess or during lunch or assemblies. Therefore, it is essential that we constantly work on those skills and behaviors that will afford them comfort, confidence, and success when the supports they have been receiving in a more restricted environment are reduced.

When the Fireflies come to PE, they only have 4–8 students on average. That won't represent their entire class because some students may be included in one of my gen. ed. PE classes. It is also common for one or two to be unable to attend even my specially designed PE class because of health or behavior issues. As small as my classes are for students with special needs, some students may require a more restrictive placement to benefit from PE, like 1:1 instruction conducted in a space with no other students present if the IEP team decides that is the best way for them to access physical education. Rather than thinking of special education and general education as two separate programs, it is more accurate to think of *all* students as general education students and of special education as a menu of services that are available to all students who need them. In the world of education, "Inclusion" is not just a desirable, it is the law.

Although most of my room 407 students only come to PE in a self-contained class, those classes follow the same units that my gen. ed. classes do. It is an important organizing principle that ensures equity. A basketball lesson or cardio challenge course will not look the same in both environments, and it shouldn't. Legally, in fact, the education program of a student who has qualified for special education services must be individualized, and that includes separate assessment criteria. Work on a wide enough variety of basic locomotor and non-locomotor skills, and your students will have a level of comfort and confidence when they join their neurotypical peers.

For those not familiar with the public education system, every school district that I know of has two job classifications for building personnel, other than administrators. Teachers are **certificated**, meaning that they have been through an approved post-secondary program, usually a graduate teacher education program at university, and earned a teaching certificate that entitles them to teach in public schools in that state. There are other staff members who work directly with students called **classified** employees. According to the Revised Code of Washington, commonly referred to as the RCW's, "classified employee" means a person who is employed as a **paraeducator** and a person who does not hold a professional education certificate or is employed in a position that does not require such a certificate."[5] While "paraeducator" is the term used in Washington State law, I've noticed that in different school systems different terms are used, such as paraprofessional, instructional assistant, and educational assistant. Also, the ways classified employees' duties are defined are different from district to district.

Think about It Questions

Ask your coworkers what labels they use for students who receive special education services. How confident are they that they are referring to their students appropriately? Do they use the same terms when speaking and writing, and if not, why not? What does the term "special education" mean to them?

Notes

1. Washington Office of Superintendent of Public Instruction, https://www.k12.wa.us/student-success/special-education, (n.d.).
2. "General Education" is not a legal or official category. It is a generic term sometimes used to refer to the mainstream student population.

3 U.S. Department of Education, Office for Civil Rights, https://www2.ed.gov/about/offices/list/ocr/docs/edlite-FAPE504.html, (July 2023).
4 I first described students as being on an "onramp" in 1999 when I was developing our district's English Language Learner Curriculum (Mokin and Goertzel, E.S.L. Onramp, in-house document). The requirement to ensure that our ELL students were appropriately supported and headed toward full inclusion with the gen. ed. population was as important to me then as it is now with our students with disabilities.
5 https://app.leg.wa.gov/rcW/default.aspx?cite=28A.150.203#:~:text=(6)%20%22Classified%20employee%22,not%20require%20such%20a%20certificate

2

Elements of Effective Instruction

The Importance of an Inventor Mindset

The most profound insight that I encountered during my teacher certification coursework occurred in the fall of 1988. I was earning my teaching credential at university, and it was probably during my second semester when we were finally getting into the nitty gritty of teaching methods. Imagine the mindset of an aspiring teacher as the day when they will enter a classroom, not as a student, but as the "boss," for the first time is only a few months away. Your anxiety only increases when you reflect that your class notes and papers are filled with theory, research, and warnings and not a single actual plan for what to do on the first day of school.

Thank goodness this methods class will answer that question. The professor had introduced the concept of lesson plan templates and examples of lesson plan parameters such as background, objectives, assessment and so forth. We were discussing the relative merits of creating one's own lesson plans versus using an off-the-shelf plan or borrowing from a colleague. "Why reinvent the wheel if you don't have to?" That was the rhetorical question the professor posed. And the answer, she said, is "We don't reinvent the wheel so we can have more wheels. We reinvent the wheel so we can have more inventors." They could have handed me my teaching certificate right then and there. It was the most profound thing I had heard up to that point and would hear until I graduated. I don't know if hearing that made me change my approach to teaching, but it definitely gave me permission to go forth and be the kind of teacher that I already was as a person.

Having an inventor mindset is one of my professional values. You will notice others as you read further. I find that professional values and personal values tend to overlap. Is there a place in the workplace for discussion of our personal values? I wouldn't have thought so until one of our principals began the first staff meeting of her first year on the subject of personal core values. She knew what hers were, and she believed it was very important for all of us to be aware of our own. Without knowing your core values, how do you teach others? How do you lead? How do you know what you stand for? What are the core values you would expect on a teaching staff? Life-long learning? Compassion? Justice? Conscientiousness? If you do not articulate your values, you are left with only job requirements and 'to-do' lists but without principles that enable you to prioritize and persist when things get difficult.

She gave us an example of the "List of Five" that she and the front office staff came up with that year. They evidently each did their own and then combined them into five they could agree on. The front office (principal, dean of students, and their executive assistants) is the administrative heartbeat of the school, and their core values might differ from a teacher's. They were: Calm, Caring, Competence, Clear Communication and Having Fun Together. Those sound like good values to live by. I wonder how the list might change if each one of those people were to do the exercise again, but with their spouses! I suppose that begs the question, "How 'core' are your 'core values?'" Are they inside so deep that circumstances don't change them, or are they domain-specific?

The need to constantly tinker with the wheel, if not actually reinvent it, is so ingrained in me that it's almost like a kind of allergy. Every time I'm given a ready-made, turnkey lesson plan, I start to "itch." Anyone who experiences a little OCD now and then knows what I'm talking about. You're in a hurry, you grab your jacket, shut the closet and head for the front door, all in one choreographed sequence, when you hear the hanger hit the floor. Who cares, you're in a hurry. And that's the moment you hesitate because you feel a strong itch or tug pulling at you that you can't ignore and won't go away until you pick up the hanger. Reading teaching manuals and other PE teachers' lesson plans sometimes gives me "the itch." I like 75% of what I see, but there is that other 25% that bothers me because I see a way it could be better (or more appropriate for my students) with a few changes. When another teacher tells me about a certain game, and it sounds fun, I'll try it using their design and rules. However, that game will be one element of a larger plan for that day, and tomorrow, when we play it again, I will have modified it more to my liking.

For me, as a former ELL (English Language Learner) teacher and now as a PE teacher, it is just so much more comfortable to write up my own plans in my own way, and that is where the inventor metaphor applies. The process one goes through when one creates, no matter what the task, has enormous value. You focus on the essence of an idea and then gradually expand it. As it expands it encompasses a small universe of connected elements. As you free your imagination, that idea encompasses images of students; it encompasses a physical space; it encompasses motion, effort, and force; it encompasses pieces of equipment; lastly, it takes on a process and sequence. Following this creative process makes me happy, and that is reason enough to do it. It also clarifies my ideas and allows me to "see" the entire lesson in my mind. My inventiveness and my intuitive abilities are taxed to the limit when I work with students who have special needs.

Because I believe that my job is important, because I believe in high standards for our profession, because I care deeply about my colleagues and students, because I am so grateful to the community that has given me a livelihood and my daughter an excellent education, I want answers to the question, "How do we nourish a culture of inventors?"

Individualized Education Program (IEP), Lesson Plans that Fit Your Students

When I plan for my Firefly PE classes, I start by thinking about my students. It is difficult to imagine an off-the-shelf lesson plan working. What I mean by that is that while lesson parameters such as warmup, focus, direct instruction, practice, activity/ game, and closing are somewhat universal, content and scope is very dependent on one's class. My students with special needs, the majority of whom in any given year have an ASD diagnosis, have individual challenges to overcome, and there is a wide range of abilities. A smaller class size coupled with added support staff allows greater liberty to create lessons that meet my students' individual needs. I refer to our curriculum texts for academic content, fitness activities, skill drills and games that I want to plug into my unit, but I rarely use an off-the-shelf curriculum without adapting it significantly. For a student receiving special education services, following their IEP is essential.

> An **Individualized Education Program (IEP)** is a written statement for a student eligible for special education that is developed, reviewed, and revised in accordance with state and federal laws. The IEP guides your student's learning while in special education. It describes the amount of time that your student will spend receiving special education, any related services your student will receive, and the academic/behavioral goals and expectations for the year.
> (Individualized Education Program (IEP), n.d., Washington Office of Superintendent of Public Instruction, https://ospi.k12.wa.us/student-success/ special-education/family-engagement-and-guidance/ individualized-education-program-iep)

IEPs are lengthy, detailed documents that may contain unfamiliar language, but do not neglect reading them. School personnel are required by law to follow these plans. They are the templates for the data and assessment teachers provide for a student. Our IEP format is standard. Here are the sections of one of my student's IEP's in order:

- Members of the IEP team, their job titles, meeting date, time, and location.

- Student and parent contact, IEP and current evaluation start and end dates.
- Cognitive goals, objectives, benchmarks, and assessment.
- Social/emotional goals, objectives, benchmarks, and assessment.
- Adaptive goals, objectives, benchmarks, and assessment.
- Strengths and Adverse Educational Impact.
- Special Factors and Accommodations specify any aids, accommodations, and modifications required for progress toward goals as well as any training/support needed for other school personnel.
- Assessment: Specifies which assessment tools are to be used in academic areas.
- Educational Services and Placement: Details recommendations for services in goal areas and other supports such as OT, PT, and SLP. This section also specifies placement considerations for Least Restrictive Environment so that the student participates with non-disabled peers in addition to special education. These would include academics, lunch, recess, assemblies, field trips, PE, music, and extracurricular activities.
- Consent forms and student information disclosure notifications to bill for reimbursement from state healthcare authorities
- Parent Input Form: your child's strengths, motivators, areas of concern, techniques useful for addressing concerns, goals for upcoming year.

Each goal area includes the names/titles of personnel who are the implementors. Because communication is such an important aspect of social/emotional behavior, the speech language pathologist (SLP) is one of the implementors for those goals and objectives. The adaptive goal implementors are the special education teacher, the general education teacher, the occupational therapist (OT) and the paraprofessional. The OT is a key player because they work with students on fine motor skills which involves everyday essential movements and behaviors such as the ability to manipulate objects, place objects in locations, open and close objects, get a drink of water, and various behaviors related to hygiene. For each of these objectives/benchmarks implementors assign a level of performance: Consistent, Inconsistent, or Partial.

In this IEP, PE is mentioned in the section, Strengths and Adverse Educational Impact, which is completed by the school's physical therapist (PT). It states that the PE teacher is to be part of consultation and monitoring regarding gross motor skills. This was the clearest point of connection to PE in the IEP. In fact, the PT was frequently present in PE at certain times of the year when she was collecting data on the student. She was not always able to witness specific behaviors she needed to evaluate, and in those cases relied on me for input on the student's goals, behaviors, and progress. The OT and PT provided me with checklists of behavior several times a year. The data they contained became part of their assessments for the next IEP follow-up. I also provided them with progress reports and comments in email form.

As a classroom teacher or specialist, you must have access and provide input to the IEP. I also find it indispensable to have at least one member of the IEP team with whom I talk regularly and with whom I have a strong working relationship. In most cases, this person would be the special education teacher as they have the most contact with my student. They understand my input is important because the gym and playing field are very different settings than a regular classroom. They expose students to different sensory input and can make them more vulnerable at times.

IEPs often contain very few specifics that look like PE goals, and that could be because the PE teacher has not been involved with the IEP process. The solution is, of course, to get involved, but in the meantime a good place for a PE teacher to find clues as to what they should work on with a student with disabilities are the adaptive and physical/occupational therapy sections of the IEP. There you will find reference to goals like delivering, balancing, and jumping. With a little imagination those can easily be incorporated into PE activities. Utilizing your paraeducators, it shouldn't be hard to differentiate or customize activity for each student in your self-contained class. However, you will want to have a unifying theme, such as, today I want to make sure we work on muscle strength, or today I want to practice taking turns and standing in lines.

Patrick is in high school now. When I knew him, he was a tall lanky eight-year-old boy with straight brown hair, a tall forehead, big friendly eyes, and a quick smile. He had a wobbly gait, and his arms moved constantly – his mouth being a frequent destination of his fingers. My image of Patrick is of a grinning excited boy heading toward me as fast as he could go. Patrick received a modified physical education program as per his IEP. Due to rights of privacy and, specifically, to the Family Educational Rights and Privacy Act (FERPA) I cannot quote language from a student's IEP. This is what his IEP could have looked like if I were to rewrite parts of it:

ADAPTIVE GOALS: To strengthen knowledge of everyday items as well as connection between objects and location.
SPECIFIC OBJECTIVES: To pick up and put down objects and foods, handle toys, to remove objects from containers and replace them, to remove and replace caps and tops on containers and pens; to walk or deliver a familiar object to a target location.
SOCIAL/EMOTIONAL GOALS: To initiate interactions with peers; to maintain appropriate distance and proximity with others; to generalize functional language across different environments.
SPECIFIC OBJECTIVES: Patrick will initiate interaction with an adult or peer in a social situation by approaching them and using a picture card or gesture, without grasping and while maintaining personal space.
GROSS MOTOR GOALS: Patrick will perform non-locomotor balance and locomotor movement traveling in different modes. Patrick will use PE equipment appropriately.
SPECIFIC GROSS MOTOR OBJECTIVES: Patrick will hold a standing position. Patrick will travel on a defined path: forward, backward speed up. Patrick will combine travel with arm movements. Patrick will pick up and carry a 4-wheel scooter and sit on it while being towed. Patrick will mimic teacher's movements with hand-held scarf and with

two-pound weights. Patrick will hold a ball, pass it back and forth with a partner, roll it back and forth with a partner.

PE ENVIRONMENT AND ACCOMMODATIONS: Patrick is to receive physical education 60 minutes per week in the school gym or other appropriate space in a smaller class designed for students with disabilities and special needs. Consultation between PT, OT and PE teacher regarding gross motor skills and mobility is to be provided.

I remind myself that special education is not a student category or a place. It is a menu of services, and each student receives accommodations tailored to their needs as specified in their IEP. These accommodations can include placement in specially designed classes taught by teachers with specific endorsements and training. They can include services provided by a PT, OT and/or an SLP. These supports serve to help students access the district's standard essential learnings. The units, if not the exact lessons, that I teach in my classes of students with special needs parallel those of my classes of neurotypical students. If this were not the case, students with disabilities who are included with neurotypical students would be at a disadvantage, being unfamiliar with the activities and lacking practice in the physical as well as the social skills required.

Paraeducators Are an Integral Part of the Team

When paraeducators, or "paras" for short, work in classrooms with students under the direction of the teacher, they perform a valuable instructional role. In our district, in the elementary school setting, paras also supervise students in the lunchroom, at recess and during school arrival and dismissal times. They are an integral part of the system. Nowhere are paras more essential than in the Firefly classroom where 1:1 support may be stipulated by the IEP team if less restrictive conditions have proven ineffective. On the other hand, removal of 1:1 adult support toward greater independence can be a growth goal for a student. When a student who has special needs qualifies for one-on-one adult support, that person is a paraeducator and not a teacher. The reason for this is that there may be four or five paras assigned to that class at various times in the day but only one certificated teacher. No one in the school gets to know the Fireflies better than the paras do. As my colleague Camille pointed out, the paras spend more "meat and potatoes time with our room 407 students than anyone else except for their parents." Now that I have worked in close partnership with numerous paraeducators for many years and watched the interactions between para and student, I know exactly what Camille meant by "meat and potatoes."

A few of my Fireflies come to gen. ed. PE, which we could refer to as "inclusion," accompanied by a paraeducator. It is a big mistake to ignore that adult, assuming that they will "take care of *their* student" while you focus on the rest of the class. First of all, they are *your* student. Second, it is only common courtesy to communicate with another educator who is in your room to help. I always find a minute to talk with the paras about the plan and the sequence for our activities, particularly when we are starting something new: size and makeup of groups, teams, stations, layout and directionality, equipment. We discuss the most important things I want to accomplish and some ideas for including/assisting any students. One of the first things to discuss is what kind of a day the student is having and if there were earlier events I should be aware of. We also use this time to talk to any of the other students who have volunteered to partner up with a student who has special needs. My paras know that they may go into the PE office any time they wish to get any equipment they need to support their student.

At the beginning of the year and any time there is a changeover in personnel make it a priority to establish a relationship of professional, mutual respect. One way of doing that is not catching people by surprise. Take the time to share the "how" and "why" of your plan with your paraeducator team before you rearrange students and ask them to switch their roles or do something new. Be aware that some of your paras may be assigned as a one-on-one to a particular student and pulling them away from that student may violate their IEP or other instructions. You want people to use their own judgment, therefore it's important to discuss the issue of autonomy. For example, my paras know that they may access the PE office and equipment whenever they need to without asking permission. Most importantly, our relationships are collegial, respectful, and friendly. They know they are free to suggest changes and propose new ideas. Teaching is hard work, and I want to be part of the kind of team where people share their best thinking.

One-to-One Instruction

How do you give a student one-to-one instruction or assistance while ensuring that teaching and learning continue for the rest of the class? The key is being prepared in advance with established routines and teamwork.

- Establish routines so that students and adults can continue teaching and learning when you shift your attention to one student. When lessons and schedules are predictable, students are more comfortable leaving the activity for temporary one to one instruction knowing what to expect when they return to the group.
- Certain students and paras are often assigned to each other and are accustomed to working together. Take advantage of that relationship.
- When a student has a one-on-one para assigned to them, and I want to step in to assist, I keep in mind that I am instructing both.
- Whenever possible, pull students out in small groups rather than individually for remediation and practice. Reserve a safe, adequate space for this, particularly when the rest of the class is engaged in intense activity. Separate the practice space with cones rather than squeezing students along a sideline or cramped corner.
- Choose your location and orientation strategically. As the teacher, when you pull out an individual or small group, choose a location and orientation that doesn't cause you to lose sight of the rest of the class.

- A large, student-friendly time-keeping device can help students perform a challenging or non-preferred task by reminding them that it is for a limited and predictable period. I may do this when I ask a student to pause a preferred activity and work on a skill with me.
- If you anticipate that some students might struggle during a game like tag, basketball, hockey or capture the flag, call their attention to the "practice zone" prior to the start of the game. Inform them that they may go there at will or on your signal, and you will be there to assist them. This is key to avoiding students experiencing frustration and alienation.

Learning Prompts

Every teacher has several ways of prompting his or her students to a task and supporting their efforts. Some prompts are more like reminders or wakeup calls. They warn us to get prepared for a task:

- Audible and visual attention-getters like clap patterns and finger-to-lips quiet signal
- Call and response lines
- Standing at a lectern
- Using proximity to signal that focus is required
- Direct eye contact
- Projecting an agenda on a screen
- Classical music

Other prompts support the task itself:

- A written template or worksheet
- Adjusting a student's grip on their pencil
- Using eye contact and gesture to signal that you are passing a ball to someone
- Modelling posture as in the "ready position"
- Demonstrating
- Providing examples

Learning prompts differ widely depending on the age of the students, the subject, the type of school, and the culture. A teacher automatically applies the appropriate prompt for the class, student, and situation. Therefore, it will come as no surprise that learning prompts used in a special education classroom will be appropriate to the needs of those students. For John, the prompt to write the letter "a" may be the letter "a" printed and followed by several blanks. For Jane, the appropriate prompt may be to place your hand over hers and guide her in tracing the letter.

Block, *A Teacher's Guide to Adapted Physical Education*, 2016, refers to levels of methodology and prompt hierarchy to explain how a teacher might approach communicating with a student with an intellectual disability or autism. The levels progress on a scale from least to most intrusive. The student:

- Responds to natural cues in environment
- Responds to verbal cues
- Responds to pointing and gestures
- Uses picture cards
- Requires demonstration
- Requires physical (hands-on) guidance

Teachers naturally try the least intrusive methods first, hoping that students will succeed on their own; if environmental cues are insufficient, they proceed to stronger cues. Fortunately, PE consistently lends itself to all levels of prompting, from environmental to physical. Activities and equipment are easily represented graphically, demonstrations are a natural part of instruction and students tend to be receptive to physical guidance when using unfamiliar equipment or performing challenging skills like batting.

The Power of Voice

I imagine that to a student, my voice in the gym is only one part of a much larger aural environment that includes all the ambient sounds, side conversations and voices in their own heads. I give a lot of thought to how my voice is perceived when I'm teaching. Why should you be any less aware of your sound when you are instructing than you would be if you were playing the violin for your students? Are you talking too much? Does your voice feel strained from talking in a high register? (If so, you can feel it in your vocal cords.) Are you taking pauses? Are you varying your tone? Are you conveying emotion? When I begin to raise my voice to be heard over students' noisy chatter, I know it is time for a pause. Instead of trying to compete with the racket, I quiet down, slow down, and try to create a contrast that is noticeable.

I am sure that I make a hundred assumptions every day about my students' comprehending my language. For the most part, I can get away with that with my neurotypical students. Even so, teachers are trained to constantly check their students for understanding by a variety of means: facial expressions, displaying work, verbal responses, raising of hands, short quizzes, and exit slips. With my Firefly students I am even more conscious of my language since I can't assume that just because I say something to them, they understand it. I learned in my ESL training that relying solely on the verbal mode when communicating is taking the "cheap way out." It blows my mind how many times I've seen ELL specialists do professional development without modelling effective communication strategies. We naturally rely on the verbal mode almost exclusively because it's quickest and easiest – but not for everyone. Every time I utilize a gesture, a written symbol, a diagram, colors, dramatic effect, or a demonstration, I know that I am reaching at least one more person in my class or audience.

When I'm with the Fireflies, I tend to stand closer to them when we talk. I shrink the interpersonal distance compared to my other classes because I try to search their expressions, look closer, and listen for all the clues that tell me we are communicating effectively. When I am teaching a student who is basically nonverbal, I find myself staring at them a lot. What is their state of mind? Are they engaged in the activity? Do they show signs of distress or boredom? When I speak to them, I give thought to the kind of voice I use, and I give even more consideration before using physical contact like a "comforting" hand on shoulder. Quotations around "comforting" because they may not perceive it as such.

Music

Music is another feature of the aural environment that many teachers make good use of. I use music in the gym every day, but I don't ever play "kids" music. You will never hear Disney soundtracks or kids' hits or contemporary earworms in my gym. They are omnipresent enough as it is. However, I invested in a high-quality sound system and do play music for specific purposes. Like many teachers, I've come to appreciate the value of music not just as a mood setter but as a learning prompt.

- I can double the time my students will do a jogging warmup or sprint relay if I play an upbeat track like Patrick Hernandez' "Born To Be Alive."
- On gloomy, low-energy days if I need to lift the mood, I like to choose something lyrical and upbeat like "In a Summer Place," or "Summer Samba." I'm a big fan of bossa nova.
- If we are doing a high-intensity workout such as a 10- or 15-minute muscle endurance station rotation, I might choose something with a heavy groove that motivates us to dig in and dig deep for stamina.
- If I want to wake my students up or change their mood because they're acting squirrelly, I like to play something unfamiliar and a little challenging like something from Miles Davis' electronic period or Thelonious Monk.

If I'm going to play music, I may as well use it as an opportunity to expose my students to the good stuff – jazz, rock, musicals, or classic cinema soundtracks. (I need to put in a plug here for the Spaghetti Western soundtracks of Ennio Morricone. Whose eyes don't open wide, and who doesn't break into a grin when they hear the theme music from "The Good, the Bad and the Ugly?!") One of the advantages of jazz is that so much of it is instrumental, so I don't have to worry about inappropriate lyrics. Picture a typical winter day in Western Washington: cold, grey, dreary. My Firefly class enters the gym. Given the time of year, it's likely one or two students are out sick, so the class is smaller than usual. Energy level is low, and we need something to brighten the mood. I might choose Bobby Darin's "Beyond the Sea" and then Julie Andrews singing "My Favorite Things." Several things happen simultaneously: Almost everyone smiles. The pace around the track quickens. The paras start to sing and put a little dance into their step. And a warmup that might have lasted three or four minutes before students got bored will now go on much longer. We cannot forget that for some of our students, managing sensory input is critical. While music is one of life's most essential sensory creations, it's not always helpful. Some students have a negative reaction to it. If a student shows distress, and you are playing loud music, that could be the cause.

I remember a student I had about ten years ago. Lydia spent most of her time, semi-reclined, in a wheelchair. She came to PE with her room 407 classmates. She was able to turn her head and move her hands and arms a little. I really had no clue at first how to include her in PE, so after talking with her teacher and support para I decided that the first step for Lydia would consist of keeping her in proximity to other students so that she could see and hear everything that went on. Once she was in proximity, we could figure out ways to involve her more fully. Keeping a student like Lydia in proximity may sound obvious; however, when a student is nonverbal and has challenged mobility, proximity doesn't happen unless someone attends to it constantly. Once she was stationed near the center of the action, we could involve her by putting a ball in her lap, which she could then push off toward a target, like a bucket or a playmate. I could substitute objects with different textures, sizes, weights and sound characteristics. We could maneuver her chair through a challenge course. So much of our efforts with Lydia involved supplying her with as wide a range of sensory inputs as possible. I don't remember how she reacted to music, but knowing what I know now, I would make sound a much more prominent part of PE for her. Not only would I experiment with different music tracks, but I would also design activities with more focus on sound effects: clapping sticks together, shakable noise-makers, scratch surfaces. I would collaborate with our music teacher to see what advice he had and look at ways we could dovetail Lydia's music and PE. We might even incorporate a collection of percussion instruments into a PE dance unit.

Your Own Inner Resources

When I remind myself that my voice is an instrument or that I need to think of language tactically, I am using my 17 years' experience as an ELL teacher. However, as helpful as specialized training is, tapping into one's own lifetime experience and using it effectively is just as important. There are certain life experiences that one draws from when one is teaching. These are experiences that may appear to have nothing to do with the job, and yet we tap into these resources when we teach. One way to look at this is that if you don't bring part of who you are to your teaching, then your students may be missing out on a vital connection to you. My daughter's third grade teacher used to work for Boeing, and she was crazy about all things having to do with airplanes. Every student she had remembers the unit in which they built model airplanes and hung them from the ceiling. Footnote: my daughter's class was the last one to get to do this because her principal decided that there was no longer any room for "pet" projects that didn't directly support the curriculum, and Ms. G's airplane unit didn't make the cut. Another teacher friend had an amazing job in a past life. She was a costume designer for the Metropolitan Opera in New York. No big surprise that her kindergarten class benefits from the wonderful projects they do with fabrics.

This may get me into trouble with some readers, but I'm hoping you will allow a comparison between animal and human behavior. I have had dogs almost all my life. My connection with dogs has found a way into my teaching, as I will explain. I've taken many of my puppies to dog training school, and I've also taken older dogs to professional trainers to work on specific problems. One thing that all dog training has in common is that it is *not* dog training – it's owner training. I am not making that up. The trainers themselves tell you that. As I took more classes and worked with my dogs, I kept getting this feeling of déjà vu, and I realized that I was being reminded of my ESL methods training. One of the main things I've learned about communicating with dogs is the importance of clarity. Commands are simple: one or two words often accompanied by a hand gesture. Reinforcement always follows in the form of a reward or a correction. You know that your dog has understood you because he has obeyed your command. Consistency of language and reinforcement is paramount. Otherwise, you confuse your dog. The command style of teaching is listed first under Standard 10, Teaching, in the Adapted Physical Education National Standards (APENS):

- Standard 10. Teaching>Understand the effectiveness of using the command style of teaching with individuals with disabilities (10.01.01.01)

How is it, exactly, that dogs have made it into my teaching? Whether you're dealing with an animal, a person who is learning a new language, or a student with sensory processing issues, you cannot rely on your everyday style of communicating. If you use idiomatic speech as you would with friends, and if you don't focus your message, you will not be understood. When I teach elementary students, I try to keep my instructions short and direct. I also try to do that with my responses to their questions and comments. If you are in a whole-class discussion, and a student makes a statement that is factually incorrect, how do you respond? Do you wiffle-waffle around the truth and try to make them feel good by couching your response in flattery? Their takeaway might be that answering a question incorrectly or without much forethought gets them almost as much approval as answering it correctly. When we are discussing anatomy or nutrition, for example, my students are eager to contribute. There are multiple hands raised wanting to share what they know or believe. However, we must get to some hard facts as quickly as possible because misconceptions are dangerous and because we only have thirty minutes to get everything done.

I could tell that I was in trouble whenever my father's voice dropped to half-volume, and he looked at me with an eerily blank expression. He was a master at setting my nerves on edge, and he did it with voice technique: lower volume, fewer words, and more space in between them. (I'm reminded of what I have read about the importance of silent space in music, particularly in jazz. Certain musicians, Miles Davis comes to mind, are known for their ability to effectively use silent space in their playing to deepen emotional connection.) This reminds me that we have untapped ways of communicating that can be developed and honed. (I will talk about a person named Ed a little later.)

I have a few ways of applying this concept of expanding the boundaries of communication. Every teacher has his or her own way of probing their inner resources for experiences and skills they can utilize to enhance their effectiveness in the classroom. I find it very helpful to monitor myself as I teach and ask myself if I'm doing the same old thing as if stuck in a groove with "tired" habits: same tone of voice, same vocabulary, same questionable quality microphone and acoustics, same speaking location, and same people doing most of the talking. On the plus side, who were the teachers that I tended to do my very best work for, and why? What did certain teachers and favorite adults do that communicated their belief in me and encouraged me to trust myself? Change and risk are good. It keeps me alert, and I am intrigued by the way it feels and to the reactions I get from my students. How exciting it is to try something new and discover that your students love it!

What Does Inclusion Look Like?

Less experienced gen. ed. teachers may view "inclusion" as more work, and, to be honest, at times it is. I know that I need to make time to monitor *any* student who I know will need a little extra attention. If I don't plan differentiated instruction in advance, I end up doing it on the fly, and that is never as effective. The key fact to remember – and I learned this a long time ago as an ESL teacher – is that the strategies I use to benefit my English language learners, my students who have processing or sensory issues, my kinetic learners, my "squirrely" kids – will always benefit everyone else even though verbal/auditory delivery may be adequate for them. Using additional strategies like **visual cues, posters, organizational systems, practiced routines, call and response checks for understanding,** or **exit slips** will serve to reinforce and cement learning for everyone. These are key inclusion strategies.

A noticeable change occurs when we place students who are nonverbal or have autism into PE classes with their neurotypical peers. They tend to pay attention and regulate their behavior to fit in with their classmates. I see it happen over and over. Here is one example. Compared to the other students in the smaller, specially designed PE class, Stevie had more athletic ability, his disability was less impactful, and his language skills were virtually at grade level. But because the other students' abilities were lower than his, it was impossible to make his physical education program challenging enough or appropriate enough. That begs the question: why was Stevie placed in a special PE class? The answer is complicated. Incidents of physical aggression toward peers, whole days of extreme behavior and/or shut down, and, unfortunately, coordinated complaints by some of the other students' parents. Due to these factors, Stevie bounced back and forth between the Firefly class and inclusion.

By fourth grade Stevie's behavior had calmed considerably. He was gradually learning the skills to self-regulate, which included being more flexible with adults and peers when he didn't get his way. Natalie, our school's instructional coach, was instrumental in this process. I watched her work with Stevie over a two-year period in PE, in the hallways, at lunch and at recess. She patiently and calmly listened, validated, questioned, and posed choices. They practiced calming techniques that involved specific language and breathing, and she regularly dropped into the gym for about ten minutes to observe. If Stevie became agitated or hostile toward a classmate, Natalie would step in and practice those behaviors with him. When Stevie was fully included, he naturally used his self-regulation skills more. Inclusion with his gen. ed. peers, the months of work with Natalie, and his classmates' openness and acceptance were the keys to his improvement and success. He learned to stay in a group or on a team, to follow the rules of the game and to give and take with teammates.

In buildings where staff are less experienced, have not been trained or have fewer supports, inclusion isn't really inclusion. It's more like co-location. Students who have special needs are placed in gen. ed. classes like PE, music, maybe science, but they do not necessarily 'participate' in the commonly accepted sense of the word. I have spoken with PE colleagues who admit that they are at a loss when it comes to including these students in many activities and that they often fall back on the convenience of leaving supervision and teaching of these students up to the paraeducators that accompany them. Are they better off being included in this way but not necessarily receiving an appropriate educational program, or would they be better off in a specially designed PE class all or some of the time? That would be an impossible choice if those were the only two options. The solution is for the staff at the school to receive training and support, preferably on site and by an experienced mentor teacher who can model effective teaching. A key here is that the training is not offsite in a conference room but in the school gym with the same students and curriculum.

When she was first included, Nanda did a pretty good job in PE when tasks were specific and non-competitive. She did well in station rotations where she was accompanied by a para and was part of a team of 3 or 4 classmates. The team stayed put in one location for several minutes and Nanda was surrounded by positive models. However, when we played competitive games like basketball or floor hockey, Nanda often retreated to a wall and sat down. I noticed this turning into a pattern when we were in our basketball unit. She and her para came to PE with a basket of books so they could pass the time reading off to the side of the gym while all the excitement, the fun, the stress of competition, and the learning happened at a safe distance. I spotted a team of two mature girls and a boy and determined to place Nanda with them. Her teammates were considerate, and even the boy, who was a very competitive basketball player, adjusted his intensity and made sure to pass the ball to Nanda. This plan and this group did very well for a couple of classes, but if I were to have made this situation permanent, Nanda's teammates would eventually have resented it. The opportunity to team with students who have disabilities needs to be given to all students.

Often, we have a transition period when a student who has been going to PE in a specially designed class attends a gen. ed. class. They may start attending that class on a regular basis or continue to attend both classes in alternating fashion. There are advantages to the latter, particularly if the gen. ed. class is engaged in a competitive sports unit for a couple of weeks. When the student attends the specially designed class, the advantageous adult to student ratio allows me to give them much more attention and to design instruction around their abilities and challenges. I try to focus on content that will help them when they return to the full inclusion class.

My Firefly class does not have the noise, crowding, and commotion that is part of a gen. ed. class of twenty or thirty students. With any student, but particularly with those who react negatively to that type of environment, there are ways to ease the transition to inclusion.

- Accompany student with a trusted adult or peer.
- Increase the amount of time in gen. ed. PE gradually.
- Allow time to experience proximity and observe.
- Encourage participation, but also pay attention to student's comfort level.
- Have a calm area and offer breaks.
- Fade adult/peer support gradually but check in periodically.

In the gen. ed. class, I do not always expect a new student to interact with a team of classmates in a game situation even when accompanied by one-on-one support, but standing on the sideline near a group while they play ball and receiving passes meets some objectives. There are ways to design this type of inclusion so that it does not feel contrived or dependent on adults constantly ordering students to include a classmate who has a disability. For example, I might include a rule that gives a team a half-point if they complete a pass to someone on the sideline. I might include a Jeopardy component in which a student on the sideline can earn a point for his team by answering a fitness or health question in lieu of a free throw. As always, one opens these special roles up to all students so that your student who has a disability does not stand out. I consider proximity with alternative participation in this situation to be a valid PE objective because the student is watching their classmates (a prerequisite to social interaction) and preparing to receive the ball. However, proximity while engaged in something entirely separate and different from everyone else is not inclusion, in my opinion.

Offering students choices is inherently an inclusive teaching strategy. If you let me choose from among options, I will select a task that is appealing and within my ability. Are you hesitant to offer choice because you think students will routinely make selections that guarantee easy success? Students may initially take the quick and easy route, but most people do not stick with a task if it is too easy, and if they see friends doing something that looks more challenging. Given exposure to a variety of choices and ranges of difficulty, students can experiment with various levels of difficulty and various features and characteristics.

A leadup activity to target/goal sports like soccer, basketball, or bowling can feature a high level of choice by offering multiple targets of varying size and at varying distances with different point values. I might design station rotations with a variety of features: rolling, tossing, putting, obstacles; and a variety of objects, beanbags, gator balls, tennis balls, medicine balls, but then be prepared to modify for students who need more support. If a student has not learned to roll or toss, let them drop the object onto the target. For a student who is most comfortable with a para or a buddy and loves to play catch, try to combine that with elements of the station rotation. For example, his partner might drop the ball into a tub after catching it, and then toss it back to him. Then both partners would get tubs and evolve the game by adjusting distances and eventually tossing into each other's tubs.

In gen. ed. PE, I have a room full of potential buddies, and therefore finding helpers and partners for students who have diverse learning needs is usually not difficult. Occasionally, it is hard to find a student to volunteer to be a buddy, but sometimes I have the opposite problem. Being a buddy can be a very popular job, and if you let them, some students will choose to be a helping buddy all the time at the expense of doing the work I have assigned. However, setting up a rotating schedule is a way to give all students the opportunity to work with a classmate who will benefit from their help. Team sport units like soccer and basketball are certainly one of the situations where you are more likely to encounter resistance to teaming with a classmate whose skills are not at their level. These activities naturally bring out students' competitive nature, and they may see a student who is unable to run fast or catch a fly ball as a handicap. Ultimately, time and experience change things for the better. If students experience inclusion in multiple settings and from kindergarten on up, it becomes natural, and all students develop adaptive skills that result from working together to find solutions.

Being the Teacher of Record

It is important to keep in mind that you, the PE teacher, are the teacher of record when students are in your class – not their classroom teacher, the behavior specialist, the autism specialist, the physical therapist, or the school psychologist. Being the "teacher of record" basically means that you oversee the students for that block of time and that you take on the responsibilities and obligations that entails. You might think that's an obvious thing to say, but a special education PE class very often has more adults in attendance than students. I have taught many classes where that was the case, not all year long, but periodically. I don't know what it is about PE classes that attracts so many visitors, but there have been occasions when my five or six students entered the gym followed by three paraeducators, the school's physical therapist, the speech-language pathologist, the district's autism consultant, the homeroom teacher, and a behavior specialist. Some of these people were familiar to me, and some I'd never seen before. Luckily, the gym is a big space!

When I first started teaching PE, I was a little intimidated by the presence of these "officials." They entered with authority and watched and observed, some without saying a word. But after a year or two I "woke up" and fully inhabited my identity as the "teacher of record," so that now when adults, other than the regular paraeducator team, accompany my classes, I walk up to them, introduce myself, and hold out my hand. And I don't walk away until they tell me who they are and why they're in the gym, and what their assignment is. If they don't have a school or a visitor's badge, I politely ask them to go to the office and get one. No one is allowed in our building without a visible ID badge. I can't stress enough how important it is for a teacher to have control over who enters and exits the classroom and to know the identity and purpose of all visitors. There are the obvious security reasons for this, but those aren't the only ones. For example, the physical therapist may be there to observe how one of her students is progressing toward objectives that are in the student's IEP, such as balance or jumping. If that is the case, it's likely I can accommodate her by inserting some of those tasks into the lesson.

Behavior consultants often act as coaches to the paraeducators who are assigned to some students. They model ways of interacting with the student, but it is not their job to support the student during the lesson. That is the para's job. I've learned to pay attention to these specialists, and I watch them closely to see what I can learn. One of our consultants is particularly interesting. She may spend 75% of the class time standing at the wall, watching, but then when she sees a teaching opportunity, she joins the para and student. She explains, steps in briefly, models, steps back, guides the para through the technique, and, when satisfied, she retreats to the wall. I have just gotten a lesson too.

Think about It Questions

Review Block's hierarchy of learning prompts on page 30. Reflect on your use of learning prompts. Do you sometimes skip over less intrusive prompts that might be effective but take some prep time in favor of more intrusive prompts that are quicker? Do you see that as a problem?

Join with several colleagues and write the names of a few students with ASD, past and present, on cards. Go around the table taking turns introducing a student and describing the steps that you and others took to accommodate them. Describe the measures that led to success and the additional measures that might be taken to solve remaining issues.

List the steps you take to help students adapt to a new inclusion situation.

How can you improve collaboration and coordination between you and your paraeducators to improve your overall teaching effectiveness?

Reflect on the ways you talk to your students. Think about the elements listed below. What conclusions can you draw about the way you communicate? Repeat the process, but this time put yourself in the shoes of a specific student and try to imagine *their* perception of the way you communicate:

- Your tone of voice
- Volume
- Grammar
- Quantity of speech (word count)
- Style (casual, formal, humorous depending on different situations)
- Pauses and silent space
- Your language and dialect. (Are you from a different country or region than some of your students, and how does that impact your language?)

3

Organization, Systems, and Routine

All the PE teachers I know who teach special education classes highly value structure and routine. It's a comfort to all students knowing what to expect when they enter the gym, gather on the circle, or sit on their number at Home Base.[1] The location itself should put us in a mindset for the target behavior. One doesn't have to think very long or hard to come up with examples of locations or rooms that tell us what we're supposed to be doing there. Think of what happens when you get behind the wheel of your car. A set of automatic behaviors immediately kicks in: set coffee in cup holder, hit the ignition, fasten the seatbelt, heat, AC etc. After teaching PE for about two years, I realized that I had been re-using certain processes over and over and that I expected my students to learn and remember them. They are basically systems or routines, and they are essential in any kind of classroom because they save time and create efficiency when they become habits.

Anchor Charts

To help my students learn and retain them, and to make sure these systems remained consistent over time, I turned each one into an **anchor chart** – a laminated poster with text and diagrams.

I have been using them ever since. A set routine when entering the gym is essential. Since most classes starts with a warmup jog, I teach the do's and don'ts of our indoor track.

- **4-cone track** This is one of the most frequently used posters at the beginning of the year with kindergarten and first and second grades. It is a diagram of the cones with the addition of arrows indicating directionality and a warning to stay outside the cones and not cut them.
- **Home Base** shows a grid of numbers on the floor in front of my teaching station where students sit. It lists four required behaviors. My fifth graders can recite these in their sleep: "Cover your number, focus your eyes, listen quietly, talk in turn."
- **Station Rotation** diagrams how groups rotate through stations and lists three key expected behaviors: "Stay with your team, rotate on the signal, follow the station numbers."

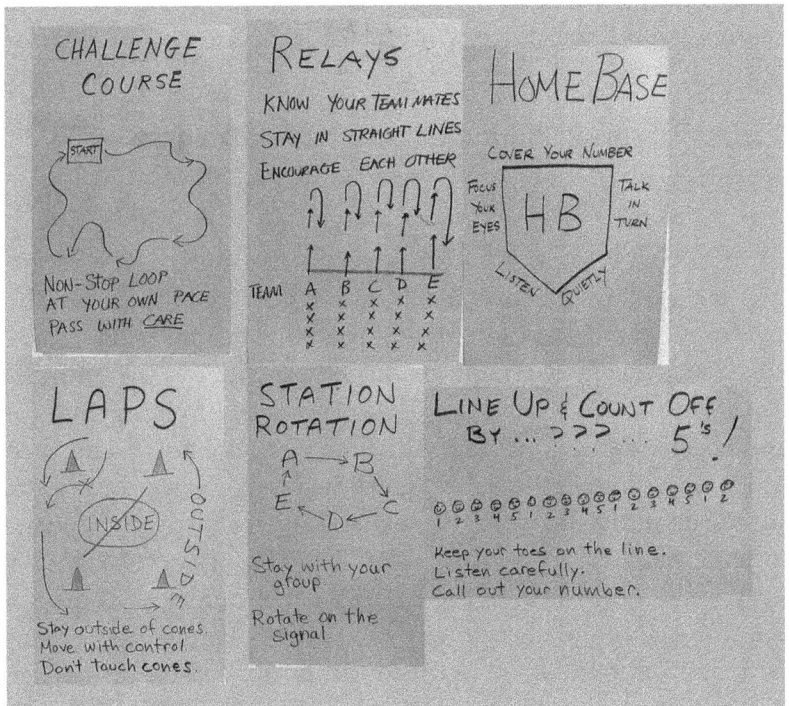

FIGURE 3.1 Anchor Charts.

Counting Off shows how students line up shoulder to shoulder and count off by a given number to create specific sized groups and lists helpful reminders: "Toes on the line, remember your number, no trading."

Relays diagrams team positions, team lines, directionality and states expected behaviors.

My gen. ed. classes assemble at Home Base after the warmup, which is where we have our discussions and do some of our direct instruction. The numbers are spaced three to four feet apart so that even my biggest fifth graders have enough room, and yet we are close enough together to be able to talk and to feel connected. There is a water fountain nearby and a large whiteboard in front of them. It is the "classroom" area of our gym. I seldom use Home Base with my Firefly classes. For one thing, we only have about six students as opposed to twenty or twenty-five. Also, I like the feeling when we gather on the twelve-foot circle in the center of the gym. We can all see each other without straining, and it feels more convivial.

Getting Prepared: Warmup, Home Base, Grouping Strategies

All my classes begin PE with a **warmup activity**. When they enter the gym, my kindergarten classes go directly to Home Base for a minute and then start their warmup, but the older grades must read the instructions on a whiteboard by the entrance. This serves several purposes. I'm in favor of anything that fosters independence, and the whiteboard alleviates the need for me to tell students what to do. It is a convenient place to diagram tasks and list warmup instructions. It's also a reference that students often return to if they've forgotten or want to double-check something such as the correct travel modes or sequence. One thing does not change, and that is the fact that all students begin with immediate activity to warm up, loosen up and get the wiggles out before I attempt any direct instruction. The three to ten minutes they spend on this gives me time to talk to any students who need my attention, need to give me parental and doctor notes, and it allows me to observe the overall mood and individual behavior. Some teachers have their classes go directly to personal space markers when they enter and begin calisthenics. One teacher I know divides her class into four or five teams, and for a week at a time each team gets the privilege of leading a set warmup routine, thus freeing her to observe and assess or prep the next activity.

Anytime you can teach your students these types of scripted behaviors it saves time and helps them become self-reliant. The more of these behaviors my students know, the more we can accomplish in our thirty minutes together because we can cut back or eliminate re-teaching and demonstrations. **Home Base numbers** are a prime example of an organizational system that we find indispensable. Students are permanently assigned a numbered spot on the floor which can be used to divide the class into teams by row, column, or evens and odds. We have equipment such as cones, tubs, buckets, balls, beanbags and poly spots[2] that match our team colors. We have class sets of pinnies (jerseys) and flag belts in multiple colors. Most schools can't afford to buy this much equipment in one season. It takes time to develop your collection, but items that facilitate organization and management should be near the top of your shopping list. Anyone who teaches primary grades knows how useful colors are in helping children see the logic and organization of a space. Here is a partial list of **grouping strategies** that I use for creating pre-set teams:

- Home Base numbers by odd/even, rows, columns, color spots
- Team choice names composed of an adjective and an animal, a muscle or a bone name
- Birthdays by month or quarter (January through March, etc.)
- Has a dog for pet, cat or bird for pet, no pet

None of these requires me to do much management. My choice depends on the size of the groups that the method will yield and on the nature of what we're about to do. I also have a few time-saving devices. My favorite is **Cleanup Crew (CC)**. CC rotates by teams for a two-week term. Crew is responsible for moving equipment, tear-down, and tidying. All my students seem to love Cleanup Crew, and they complain when another team gets more work than they had.

Pair groups are required for many activities and tasks, and there are many ways to create partners. Unless your real intention is to have students partner with their best friends, letting them select their partner is not generally a good way to go about it. I have watched groups of boys and girls spend literally *all* their remaining game time squabbling over who gets to be whose partner. I have found that the best partnering methods are those that give students and teacher some say in the outcome. The one I have used most often is **"Will You Be My Partner?"** After the class is gathered in one area, you instruct your students to mingle and ask a classmate, "Will you be my partner?" The rule is that you must respond, "I'd be happy to be your partner," unless you have already promised someone else. When everyone is standing with a partner, the teacher surveys the class to see if they are satisfied with the partnerships. If yes, then they call out, "I'd be happy to be your partner," and that settles it. If for any reason the teacher does not approve of one or more of the partnerships, then they announce, "Sorry, not today, maybe some other day." Then, *after all the groans and complaints*, all students repeat the process and look for their second choice. I almost never agree to the first choices just so students stay in the habit of being flexible. This process not only allows me to head off partners who will be disruptive, but also makes it easier to include students who are not normally anyone's first pick. I also avoid having to single out one pair of students for making a choice I don't approve of.

Routines and Scaffolds Benefit Diverse Learners

All special educators I have met agree on the importance of using some type of **visual schedule**. Like many learning issues, you cannot take it for granted that every student comprehends that class has a finite beginning and end as well as a sequence of activities that need to be followed. If I do not provide a consistent way for them to see the sequence of expected tasks, some students can become anxious. Not only is a visual schedule board essential for students' learning, but consistently following it reassures students that reality meets their expectations. I have used several different styles of visual schedules in the gym, but eventually I settled on these features for my students with special needs:

- A durable laminated poster that is easy to read and can be quickly attached and detached from the wall
- All numbers, photos and captions mounted with Velcro
- Large numbers to denote sequence
- High-quality photographs of activities/tasks featuring our students in our gym

It took some time to arrive at the best ways of using the schedule board with my students. I found that there was almost no such thing as being too methodical with the Fireflies, whether they were in our special PE class, or in gen. ed. The more that we referred to the schedule during our lesson, the better my students were at following our agenda. This was the process we found most effective to facilitate transitions:

- On entering the gym, students go to the schedule, touch the number, one, and say it aloud, touch its photo and say the task, such as "track," point to the track.
- Students go to the track, touch the cone labelled "1" and repeat "one."
- Start the task.
- When it is time to transition, I take the schedule off the wall and bring it to station 1.
- I say, "schedule board," and wait for students to gather. We repeat the same process with stations 2, 3 and 4.

Here is a question. Have you ever collaborated with your school's Speech Language Pathologist (SLP)? I must admit that I didn't for many years. That doesn't mean we weren't on friendly terms.

FIGURE 3.2 Visual Schedule.

We just never collaborated on work product until one day Camille suggested that our SLP would probably make a schedule board for PE. That never occurred to me, and when I asked her, she said she would be happy to do it. Not only that, but she had several excellent questions about size, style, and content that helped me to focus on exactly what I wanted to accomplish – a perfect example of the value of collaborating. Our SLP took the activity and student photo files I sent her and created a communication board that was custom made for our students, our activities, and our gym. She also made smaller versions for individual students who needed the reassurance of knowing at any given time where they were supposed to be, what was coming next, and when class would be over. When I mounted the large picture poster schedule on the whiteboard next to a written agenda, which version do you think the neurotypical students checked most often? The picture poster. Again, the pictures, anchor charts, and graphic references that I use benefit many more students than those one or two who may absolutely depend on them.

When my Fireflies come to gen. ed. PE, they have a Home Base number like everyone else. They may also bring an iPad outfitted with communication software or a fidget. Knowing that Camille and our other special education professionals focus on routine and schedule with their students, I try to emphasize those elements. When I write the agenda or task list on the board, I break it down into short components. I draw a box next to each item, and when we complete it, I draw a check mark through it. In room 407, I've noticed that students have different devices for tracking transitions. For example, they might move a marble from one box or compartment to another when they transition from one activity to another. Their learning tools are in containers that have specific locations on a shelf. A lot of thought goes into the organization of the physical space and the location of every object. That way students know where their tools are, and they know the process for cleaning up and putting them away when they are done. I can't think of a command that gets better compliance in Firefly PE, than "Time to clean up!" The Fireflies are always striving for independence!

Teachers know that transitions tend to be opportunities for disruption and off task behavior and that anything one can do to tighten them up is worthwhile. A big part of that is ensuring students know where they are in the task order and follow it, so that teachers' repetitive correcting is eliminated. One of Love and Logic's basic principles[3] is to not engage argumentatively with students. The idea is to make the rules and logical consequences the "bad guy," not you. I don't say it aloud, but when students try to argue out of a task or transition, I adopt an attitude that conveys, "I'm very sorry, Bethany, but it's out of my hands. These are our rules." Consistent use of a well-designed schedule board is one of the best tools for avoiding problems.

Some routines and systems depend on your location: indoor, outdoor, classroom, gym, multi-purpose room, or lunchroom. When I had classes in the lunchroom, before and after lunches, there were unique safety issues. The room was not only smaller than the gym, but tables, garbage cans, and a stainless-steel refrigeration table lined the walls. Basketball court lines were painted on the floor, but it was a smaller court, and the sideline area was half the width of the one in the gym. A "safety" anchor chart highlighted danger areas and included warnings about not climbing under furniture to retrieve balls. An itinerant PE teacher would have unique challenges. Your space is likely different at each location you travel to. You might have routines and student jobs related to travelling and carrying equipment. Anytime I travel with a class between the gym and the field, I must account for the time that takes in my lessons. Therefore, I need to teach students my expectations around travelling through the halls and responding to my signals to stop play, cleanup, and lineup. I allocate the first two weeks of every school year for teaching and practicing

- Fire drills
- Lockdown drills
- Earthquake drills
- Appropriate behavior while walking in hallways
- Entering and exiting the gym
- Bathroom and water fountain rules

The Track: A Mobile Learning Platform

The track is not just for jogging or running. It is a learning platform that happens to be in motion. We can transfer many of the skills that we learn standing still to the track. In fact, when I start a basketball unit with young students, I don't have them dribble in place. Confining a bouncing ball to a small area is too hard for most of them, and it's less intimidating when they're already moving freely. I wait until they have been jogging and doing animal walks for a few minutes, and then I have them grab a basketball from the cart and just keep going. That way it's a continuation of a familiar activity with a little fun added to it. Trying to get kindergarteners or first graders to assemble and remain on spots, deal with personal space, and manage the inevitable squabbles over who gets to be next to their friend can strain the limits of everyone's patience! The other reason to accustom students to learn ball skills while on the track rather than standing still is that every game and sport I can think of requires ball handling while on the move.

Thus, we teach and reinforce anchor systems like the Track, the Learning Circle, Home Base, Station Rotations, and then we introduce movement and equipment. After that, the students are comfortable when we substitute different tasks and equipment.

Station Rotations

Because it is such a versatile learning method, I use **Station Rotations** consistently. I design them around a theme like muscle strength or hand–eye coordination, or around a piece of equipment to practice exercises that I have just introduced. It is a lesson with usually four to six locations, or stations, spread out, each with its own equipment and each numbered or lettered to facilitate the correct rotation order. You can adjust the size of your teams by changing the number of stations. I use an interval timer app that displays a countdown timer projected on the wall. I can also run music from my playlist through the app. Students benefit because they can see how much time is left before they rotate. It is more effective and fun than just blowing a whistle every three minutes. I've emphasized the importance of mirroring my gen. ed. PE units in Firefly PE, but the latter will have modifications. For example, when my gen. ed. classes did a "game skill"-themed rotation with stations for long rope, scarf juggling, magnetic darts, shooting baskets, and scooters, I made some substitutions for the Fireflies. I substituted beanbags and tubs for basketball, and instead of a long rope, which would occupy two adults just to turn it, we walked and hopped through an agility ladder. Those simple modifications still met my skills objectives for tossing to a target and for agility. There were a lot of transitions in this lesson, and a key look-for is that my students follow the guidelines on the anchor chart as these represent **behaviors that promote learning** (one of two subsections in our report card): Stay with your team, rotate on the signal, follow the station numbers. The other subsection is **skills and concepts**. When a station is difficult for a student, we modify. Patrick was able to participate at every station with Chandra's support. For example, he had not yet been successful at learning how to throw or toss, so instead I had him walk to the tub and drop his beanbag in, and he brought his dart to the magnetic target and stuck it on – thus practicing one of his IEP goals, which was to associate an object with a target location.

Think about It Questions

Copy the following table and list the grouping and team formation strategies you use. Rate each one on a scale of 1–4 (low to high) in terms of the following values: frequency (how often used), ease of use, adaptability (can be adjusted to yield different results), and inclusiveness (accommodates diversity and doesn't cause shame).

STRATEGY	FREQUENCY	EASE OF USE	ADAPTABILITY	INCLUSIVE

FIGURE 3.3 Grouping Strategies.

If you use a visual schedule, can it be improved? If you are not using one, what are the elements that you would include, and how would you use it?

Notes

1 I painted a grid of numbers on our gym floor facing the whiteboard. The grid has six rows with five numbers per row that mark seat locations for my classes. Numbers are spaced far enough apart to give each student a comfortable personal space to sit.

2. Poly spots are pliable, multi-color rubber discs about ten inches in diameter. We use them to mark personal space locations on the floor, as bases, or as foot marks in an obstacle course.
3. Love and Logic is a parenting and classroom management approach that gives children the power to make choices and live by their consequences. Through empathy, mutual respect, and elimination of power struggles, a calmer more productive classroom environment can be created.

4

Understanding Behavior, Sensory Diversity, and Challenges to Engagement

There is always a group of students who come to us alert, well-fed, with access to resources and supported by parents who are committed to education for their children and for themselves. For those students, it almost doesn't matter how we present content to them. They will learn and thrive despite everything we do. However, for a growing number of students, we cannot take learning readiness for granted. Their stomachs are growling, there are few resources in their home, they spend hours alone because their parents are working. As teachers, we are familiar with families who are even worse off. Their challenges are overwhelming: homelessness, food insecurity, abuse, illness, and loss of parent. The challenges are compounded for families of students who have disabilities. There is research showing that the incidence of trauma among people with disabilities is higher than for the neurotypical population. According to the National Child Traumatic Stress Network, children with intellectual and developmental disabilities appear to be at an increased risk for physical abuse, physical restraint and seclusion, sexual abuse, and emotional neglect.[1] In his book, *The Body Keeps the Score*, Bessel Van Der Kolk describes the trauma that results when relationships that we depend on are severed and betrayed in the form of abuse and neglect. The contextual framework for this book is trauma, and he presents a clear explanation of humans' evolutionary dependence on relationships for survival and for a sense of basic safety.

Connecting with Students Who Have Special Needs

There are some children that you do not immediately warm up to. And that is an understatement. On the other hand, there are those students whom I've taught for scarcely a year and would not hesitate to bring home after school and present to my wife, declaring, "Hon, we're adopting Clara. Her parents said it's okay." What is it about Clara or Lester or Siddharth that your

FIGURE 4.1 Encouraging Perseverance While Giving the Option of a Helping Hand.

gut tells you, "Yup, this kid gets me, and I get them." The qualities in our children, siblings (sometimes), closest friends, and spouses (hopefully) that endear them to us are the same qualities that we discover in many of our students. Or not. Teachers do not have to love their students or even like them. That is not what we are paid for. However, it definitely streamlines the teacher–student relationship if we do not have to fight our way through our own negative impressions in order to connect with the learner within.

Like most teachers, I realized early in my career that the teacher–student relationship is critical to learning. In 1938, the philosopher John Dewey argued that progressive education needed to depart from the authoritarian model of the past where knowledge was handed down intact from educator to student. His progressive model described a reciprocal relationship in which teachers take learners' experience and background into account to create an interactive and effective learning environment.[2] Dewey didn't go so far as to say that teachers needed to develop a bond with their students, but one can infer that a teacher who strives to incorporate students' personal experience into their teaching is probably someone who has respect for their students and cares about them. In the educational context, the word "relationship" encompasses an enormous inventory of pedagogical layers as well as social-emotional content. Without having the answers to several questions about their students, a teacher cannot meaningfully teach. For example, what can I assume about my new third grader, Samantha? For sure, I can assume she knows about raising her hand when she wants to talk in class. I can assume she knows about staying in line when the class walks down the hall. I can assume that by now she's comfortable working in small groups. Actually, I can't assume *any* of those things. Samantha's family is from India. When she's with her family everyone cross-talks over each other, and that's normal to her. Maybe her previous teachers had all their desks in rows and columns, and they almost never did groupwork. In some Asian countries, volunteering a comment is frowned on, and asking challenging questions of the teacher is viewed as poor behavior.[3] Of course, it takes time to get these and other answers about your students, but a teacher needs to embark on that discovery process early on.

When we transplant the notion of teacher–student relationship into the context of a student who has autism, who may be nonverbal, or who may have an intellectual disability, it feels like a different world. Unless you have grown up with such a person in your family, it feels very unfamiliar. As a PE teacher who only sees their students twice a week, it is going to take time to get to know my students. Unlike an elementary classroom teacher who spends most of every day with the same 20 or 25 students, I see over 400 students in a week. I've taught many of them from the time they were in kindergarten to fifth grade. That certainly gives me a long-term familiarity with them, but simply having a child in my class for six years is no guarantee that I get to know them. I have an average of eight classes a day, and sometimes it seems like a train schedule. Believe it or not, an actual conversation of more than four sentences is rare, and when I am able to find the time to chat with a student about things in general, and they are willing to chat with me (which is not always the case), it is a memorable event in my day.

Behavior Is Communication

I can't walk in the shoes of a person who has autism, and because so many of my students are also nonverbal or nearly so, they do not tell me what they are thinking or feeling. At times emotions are obvious: smiles, claps, laughter, tears, and crying. At other times, we construct hypotheses based on the many behaviors, signs, and signals that we observe. The staff who work with students with disabilities all day are proficient at reading students' emotional state, including the signs that often lead up to behavior escalation. They also develop a pretty good understanding of the causes and triggers. They understand that students do not just melt down out of the blue for no reason. The cause may not be clear to us, but we must believe that there is a reason. To me, the special education paras' and teachers' ability to identify their students' triggers and motivations verge on being magical. The behavior that strikes me as random is logical to them because they know their students better than I do. In fact, what they know, and what I have come to learn is that **"behavior" is communication**. It is less of a mystery to them because they recognize the triggers or antecedents. Talk to your colleagues and learn everything you can about your students. Also remember that familiarity and interaction are not the only ways to learn about your students. Individualized Education Programs (IEPs), and, in some cases, Functional Behavior Assessments (FBAs), are critical resources that the IEP team has developed, and they contain information that you need to know.

Everyone has their own set of triggers that cause anxiety and stress. These are some of the things that trigger my students' behavior escalations: not getting what they want, having to stop doing something that they like, having to leave a place where they are comfortable, having to work when they don't feel like it, wanting to go home, wanting their mom and, of course, not feeling well. Then there is the category of causes related to trauma and deprivation that have been labelled ACEs: Adverse Childhood Experiences. Every student body has a percentage of students with these. I have a student in room 407 now who has ACEs, and I find this particularly sad.

If you didn't know Kayden, and you met him for the first time, you might think: "There's a very watchful, observant, and thoughtful-looking young man." He would sit on the gym floor against the wall, legs folded, arms in lap, leaning forward and quietly watching. I might walk up to him and say, "Kayden, are you ready to walk laps with me?" and he would reach out and pinch my leg. Unfortunately, Kayden had a pattern of communicating discomfort, disagreement, and avoidance through physical means. This only had to occur once for me to change my approach. When Kayden sat against the wall taking a break with his support para, I learned not to approach him directly before checking with the para first. We discussed whether he needed more time or was ready to resume activity, and that resulted in fewer uncomfortable situations for him and less unexpected behavior.

Behavior Triggers (The World of Unexpected Things)

We depend upon predictability, and we flounder in randomness and chaos. To varying degrees, we are all creatures of habit, and we like our routines and personal surroundings to be stable – coffee pot and toothbrush in the same place, car that starts, news at six o'clock, family all present and accounted for. Personal items stay where we left them and don't move around during the night. But imagine if they did. How disoriented, how frightened, how crazy would you feel? I know that some of my students have a particularly bad reaction to the unexpected. What made Kayden's outbursts so unpredictable to me is that his world of "unexpected things" was much larger than I comprehended. His behavior escalation could be sudden and scary and really did seem to arise out of the blue. I knew that he was one of the many students who needed lots of repetition before I introduced something new, and I knew he was not a fan of change. What I didn't know and never really got a handle on was, **what seemed insignificant to me was actually a very big deal to him**. Looking back, I believe this is one of the most important lessons a teacher needs to learn, and the learning is continuous.

While I know that Kayden could have a bad reaction to change, I have always been curious what unwanted change *felt like* to him. I am just guessing, but perhaps it is like that feeling of disorientation and terror you would experience if you woke up and saw that your coffee pot, your toothbrush, your shoes and all your furniture had moved during the night. If that is too ridiculous to relate to, another example from real life might offer insight, but again, I am just searching for a way to get inside of my student's head.

Have you ever had the experience of parking your car in a crowded parking lot; you've come to a complete stop, and you think you have set the brake when suddenly you start rolling forward toward the rear bumper of another car? You reflexively stomp on the brake, and then in a head-swimming flash of realization you see that the car next to you has started to back up, and within your visual frame of reference your brain had no evidence to the contrary, so you experienced it initially as your car moving forward until you look up and see it is an illusion. In the meantime, you experience momentary dizziness and panic that you are about to hit the car in front of you. That illusion caused by totally real outside stimuli even induced a physical response over which you had no control. Stomping on the brake, like all reflexes, was beyond the reach of your executive function, and that is as it should be. However, another person's reflex might just as easily be screaming or punching the steering wheel. It helps me to try to imagine what is going on inside a student's head when their behavior escalates, and they act out. I remind myself that I have experienced temporary sensations of dislocation and panic, and that there were real, tangible causes behind those feelings.

Over the three years I taught Kayden PE, I never completely let down my guard around him. I had two major worries. First, that he would seriously injure someone, and that included myself. The second was that I did not know if I could trust my own reaction if he really hurt me. If I were to push or strike a student for *any* reason, I am sure there would be hell to pay, and that my job and even my teaching certificate would be in jeopardy. This is why Right Response training,[4] or something equivalent, is so important. You learn to focus first on prevention and de-escalation, and only when those methods are not sufficient to keep a student safe, do we resort to physical intervention. You learn how to safely restrain and escort a student when their safety depends on it. There are so many scenarios and so much to remember that I know I won't retain everything. I just hope that if I must step into a situation, I will remember enough and that my instincts won't let me down. Just like First Aid/CPR, Right Response certification must be renewed every few years. I had to admire how relaxed Kayden's support paras were with him. They stood next to him, held him without hesitation or apparent concern. When you develop a relationship based on familiarity and trust, you and your students benefit.

When Dawn worked with Kayden, and if he was doing something enjoyable, he conveyed his happiness by smiling, dancing, and engaging in the activity with enthusiasm. When she or his teacher asked him to do something that he did not want to do, he communicated his unhappiness by whining and looking unhappy. When he worked with those trusted adults, he tried to comply even though he looked very uncomfortable. You could see him making the effort, and it was clear he wanted to cooperate. When the demands on him continued to the point where his patience was exhausted, he resorted to communicating his refusal by physical means. I watched these kinds of interactions many times, hoping that Kayden wouldn't be pushed to that point. When I worked with him, I was careful to gauge his mood so that I could back off or offer him a sensory break when it looked like his behavior was escalating. His sensory break menu for PE contained a few options: 1. Leave group activity and join a single partner. 2. Go to Dawn. 3. Go to wall and sit for 5 minutes. Sometimes Kayden did not ramp up gradually, or perhaps I just missed the signs he was expressing. However, Dawn and Camille had no problem "pushing" Kayden to work and to follow teacher's instructions because they were so accustomed to interacting with him. They also rewarded him when he completed his work by allowing him to engage in his preferred activity which tended to be sitting down in a quiet place and watching. My first goal with Kayden was for us to feel comfortable around each other and to develop trust. I would achieve that through proximity, routine, kind language and by adopting a more laid-back posture toward him than with my other students.

 The Fireflies are in the middle of a basketball unit. I've lowered a basket to minimum height, about seven feet, and dragged over a metal tripod hoop that is even lower. The students start shooting hoops, but Dawn accompanies Kayden to the wall, where he sits down as told and quietly watches for several minutes. The other students are engaged, and I would like Kayden to try to join the group. I walk toward Dawn and him while dribbling a ball and stand about eight feet away. "Come on Kayden, let's shoot some hoops." I know that Dawn has him chilling for a reason. She may have judged that he was not ready to join the whole group, or she may have sensed that his behavior was potentially escalating and therefore decided to allow him some alone time. However, it's been a few minutes, and I would like him to try to participate. Dawn tells him to get up, which he does. Then tells him to "follow Teacher," and with me leading, we head toward one of the baskets. I start to shoot and encourage him to come closer. He and Dawn are in front of the basket. I hand him the ball, and, as I reach out, he takes a swipe at my face and grazes my cheek with his fingernails. Luckily, I am just far enough away to avoid a serious cut. I know when my presence is not helpful. I leave the ball with Dawn and join the other students until it's time to clean up. PE is over.

Later in the day I saw Dawn in the staffroom and asked her about the incident. Did she have any idea why Kayden reacted the way he did? She shrugged and said, "It's difficult to say. Maybe he just wasn't ready to do something different." I thought about it off and on over the next few days leading up to our next class. Dawn didn't have anything else to offer on the subject, and it didn't seem like much to go on. But the more I thought about it, the more truth her statement seemed to contain. Kayden had done well for the first twenty-five minutes of class. It was only at the very end that his behavior escalated. We had successfully navigated through at least half-a-dozen activities without mishap. Maybe that was Kayden's limit. Perhaps, getting him back on his feet, bringing him to a basket among lots of other active bodies and me putting a ball in his face was just too much! It may have been too much work, too much proximity, and too much change.

Instead of ruminating on what happened and why, I wish I'd had a more productive means of debriefing the event so that Kayden's teachers could have learned from it, and he could have benefited. Our front office has incident/accident report forms for staff to fill out when something happens at work, but these are to provide evidence in case a claim is filed. To learn from the incident with Kayden, I would have had to get answers to some specific questions. This is the kind of tool that would have been useful.

What happened before the incident?
- What task was the class engaged in?
- How was it introduced?
- What tools/equipment were used?
- Who was present?
- Where did it take place?
- What was the student doing?
- Describe the sensory aspects of the environment.
- Do you know what the student's day was like before they entered your class?

Describe the incident:
- What did the student do?
- Was anyone else involved?
- Was anyone injured?
- What did you do?
- What were you feeling?
- Was the lesson interrupted? If so, for how long?

What happened after?
- Did you need to take measures to calm and reassure the students?
- How long was it before teaching and learning resumed?
- How long did you wait before talking to someone about the incident?
- Who did you talk to about it?
- How did they help you?

Who needs to know about this?

What did you learn?

FIGURE 4.2 Student Incident Reflection Tool.

Hiking and Eloping

The Fireflies always started with a walking warmup around four cones in the gym, and then we did backwards walk, "Look over your shoulder!" and side slides, "Face the circle…now face the walls!" Then we changed to animal laps – elbow out like a chicken, elephant trunk with arms out in front and hands overlapped, monkey – arms grabbing at pretend tree branches, eagle – arms out wide and soaring. During the warmup our paras walked or jogged alongside their assigned students, encouraging, and supporting, while I led the parade and joined up with each student in turn, offering more help and encouragement. However, not all the class would participate. It was common for one or two students to run off on their own to a corner or to climb on the mats. Some students habitually headed for the exit door, and that would cause one of us to immediately sprint in pursuit. I first met Romy when she was in the second grade. She came to PE with her classmates, a small group of five to seven students. Because of the level of support required for her to access an educational program, she had a fulltime one-on-one paraeducator assigned to her. Romy was a hiker, although the technical term is "elopement behavior." She liked to keep moving, and whether she was in the gym or outside on the playing field, she gravitated toward the perimeter and walked purposefully while flapping her hands and snapping her fingers. I thought of Romy's behavior as "hiking" as opposed to "elopement" because she did not attempt to exit the gym but only the immediate instructional area. Moreover, it appeared to me that she sometimes just needed more space or a short sensory break and did not wish to discontinue the task entirely. Walking and "wandering" enables some students to focus and process and does not necessarily signal that learning has discontinued. If we were doing our warmup laps around four cones, Romy would often continue moving but follow a path close to the walls, thus putting distance between herself and everyone else. Proximity to the wall may have comforted her. Perhaps it provided structure and solidity that helped Romy to stay oriented spatially and/or emotionally. If we were at the Learning Circle doing balances or step boxes, she might leave her spot and stroll to other parts of the gym while engaging in hand stimming movements, but then she often returned to the instructional area on her own. Whether the activity itself was non-preferred or proximity to the group was non-preferred was difficult to know without collecting more data. Romy's Behavior Intervention Plan (BIP) was not in place until her second year at school at which point, we had a logical game plan, and it was easier to maintain consistent strategies in her different environments – special education classroom, general education classroom, PE, and music.

Two Helpful Tools: Functional Behavior Assessment & Behavior Intervention Plan

There are two documents that are sometimes required with students like Romy, in addition to the IEP. These are the **Functional Behavior Assessment (FBA)** and the **Behavior Intervention Plan (BIP)**. The FBA is a detailed assessment of the behavior – not just the what, when, and where, but also the why, as best as can be determined. The BIP details the plan for addressing the behavior. Fran had a pocket-full of half-sheets of paper that she sometimes filled out during PE. It was data-keeping that was required by Romy's BIP. She mentioned that back in the classroom there were stacks of these half-sheets. Each time students with BIP's exhibited "target" behavior she had to document the "A,B,Cs" on one of those papers: What was the *A*ntecedent: Was there a demand? a transition? a fire drill? What was the *B*ehavior: Elopement? Refusal to work? Self-harm? What was the *C*onsequence: Did you reissue the demand? Remove the demand? Change the request? Use proximity? Step away?

When behaviors are a concern to staff and/or parents, the IEP team may call for assessment of the behaviors which may result in an FBA and a BIP. According to the Washington Office of Superintendent of Public Instruction, Division of Special Education, a "good FBA will look beyond what the behavior *is* to what the behavior *does* for the child" (*Special Education in Washington State: A Handbook for Parents and Educators*, 2016, pp. 29–30). Looking at what the behavior 'does' for a child may be a novel concept if we are stuck in the habit of thinking about negative behavior as something to be controlled or disciplined. Once we accept that *behavior is communication*, then we no longer look at tantrums and harming in a disciplinary context. According to the Handbook, experts say there are only two functions for the behavior:

1. to get something (attention, sensory stimulation, status, rewards, power), or
2. to escape or avoid something (pain, boredom, anxiety, fear, someone not liked)

When Romy reached third grade, her **BIP** was in place. The **target behavior**, or behavior that was negative and needed to be discontinued, was "eloping from the assigned area or instructional space without permission." While elopement was not her most disruptive behavior (those were self-harming and screaming), it was the target behavior identified by Romy's IEP team, and it did occur more frequently. The **desired behavior** was for her to "maintain an appropriate learning posture, independently completing all preferred and non-preferred tasks, without eloping from the area." The **replacement behavior** proposed was "instead of engaging in the target behavior, Romy will request a sensory break from the non-preferred task." Even though specialists approach instruction somewhat differently than classroom teachers, I still thought that was something I could work with in PE. We think in terms of half-hour chunks. There is no extending or resuming an activity after 30 minutes is up. It might be four days until I see my students again, and then another three days after that. I would not have to implement all the instructional procedures that they used in the classroom, but I could certainly implement those that fit within a PE context and timeframe, and I believed we could come up with a practical list of replacement behavior options.

The **functional explanation**, or hypothesis, of the purpose for Romy's target behavior was task avoidance. Our goal was to have her return to the task as soon as possible after a break and to learn to request breaks proactively instead of resorting to eloping behavior. Therefore, we needed to create a menu of activities that would satisfy her need for a sensory break and provide PE alternatives that made sense within the lesson. Romy's classroom teacher and I collaborated on several PE additions to the PECs (Picture Exchange Communication System) that she would use to communicate her preference of sensory break options:

- Walk laps
- Walk laps with weighted blanket
- Bounce basketball
- Use a sit-and-bounce ball
- Roll or bounce on gym mat or incline wedge
- Water fountain

I hoped that if Romy chose to use the weighted blanket, at least we could encourage her to walk with it. I wanted Romy's sensory breaks to involve some locomotor or non-locomotor movement. Some of the items on the sensory break menu in her BIP, such as bubbles and hammock chair, could only be used when Romy was in her classroom, but the weighted blanket could be brought to the gym if it proved necessary. With the BIP in place, we felt more confident in our ability to help Romy reduce the target behavior and return to task. The FBA and BIP are two important tools in the Positive Behavior Support (PBS) toolkit, discussed later. Block (2016) includes detailed templates of both (pp. 312–314). Whether or not you teach students who have IEPs, you have students who exhibit a wide range of challenging behaviors.

Repetitive Movements and Vocalizations

Romy had several behavior patterns that seemed to be inwardly directed. In other words, they didn't appear to be communicative or social in nature but instead seemed to serve a self-regulatory purpose. Some of us chew our fingernails, tug on an earlobe, or vibrate a leg while seated. Romy had an unusual and repetitive habit that involved her PECs. She brought her PECs with her when she came to PE, and she would use them to show me when she wanted certain things: to go to the bathroom, to get water, to return to the classroom. Each of these was represented by a different card. She would take one of these cards and rapidly flap it against her tooth (always her right incisor.) After a few seconds she would extend her arm straight and continue to flap the card in the air. She often repeated this cycle several times before showing it to me. I learned that I couldn't rush this process. Sometimes she showed it to me for a split second but not long enough for me to see what it was before returning to the behavior. Eventually, she would hold it still for me. Sometimes she just circled the perimeter of the gym flapping the card and never presented it to anyone. When I asked one of the paras about this, she replied, "Oh, she's stimming." When I asked her what that meant, she said that it was self-stimulation behavior. "And the purpose is...?" I asked. "Well, it seems to calm her. It could be an outlet for energy or anxiety."

Some students' vocalizations are speech-like. It sounds almost like they are quietly rehearsing lines from a play over and over. I have a feeling that many students who vocalize repetitive speech have spent a lot of time in front of a TV and are absorbing sounds and speech that they repeat with excellent intonation throughout the day. It seems that the repetition of sounds may give comfort and focus. It reminds me of echolocation. When I repeat my language it announces my presence, and others respond. That puts a social spin on it, but, in fact, it may simply be that the person is delay-echoing speech they've heard earlier, or their own words. The technical term for this is "echolalia." Romy's vocalizations were strident, urgent, and at times alarming, and she often accompanied her vocalizations with arm and hand movements. She flexed and extended her arms, did finger and hand snaps.

Protecting a Student's Dignity and Modesty

A concept that I've heard special educators refer to often is the need to "preserve a student's dignity," or "preserve their modesty." If the tables were turned, would you want a big person putting you in a bear hug or restraint hold if they could prevent you from hurting yourself by simply standing between you and the wall or by interposing their hand? I remember the first time I saw a paraeducator do this when a student was banging his forehead with his fist. She gently put one arm around the student's shoulders and placed her other hand, palm outward, against his forehead, thus shielding him from the blows. That was an insightful moment for me because it so clearly revealed that the less we restrain, force, or immobilize a student, the more their dignity is preserved. It's also common sense that the more force that is applied, the greater the chance of injury to both student and teacher. Anywhere in the school, when staff resort to physically handling students for their own safety, one of those present must have gone through Right Response training, and that adult should be directing the situation.

We need to be familiar with our school's and/or district's safety policies regarding restraint or physical contact with students. When a student harms themselves or others, our school district policy calls for an adult to intervene to protect, in which case physical restraint is allowed. When these events occur, my thinking brain kicks in quickly as I try to determine what to do next to keep students safe and calm so that learning can continue. Many thoughts flash through my mind. "What's the best way for me to help? Should I assist the para who is trying to calm a student whose behavior has escalated? What would the student's parents do in this situation? What do I do in the meantime with my other students? What would their parents think if they were watching? What is the playbook when one or more students' unregulated behavior affects the class and disrupts learning? I try to

- Make the area safe.
- Model calm and attend to students' needs.
- Resume teaching and learning.

There are many ways to facilitate returning the class to a positive, productive state.

- Escort a student to a place where they can regulate their behavior.
- Move the class to a different location in the learning space.
- Transition to the next activity.
- Take a timeout to talk, sing or do a fun game.
- Recognize that your students may have an emotional reaction and may want to talk or ask questions.

I think it's important to recognize the emotional component to teaching, particularly when situations are unsettling or disturbing. When a student harms self or others, I have an emotional reaction, and the emotions someone else feels are specific to them. The emotions can be powerful, and when time permits, I always discuss the event with one of the paras or later in the day with the student's teacher.

Managing the Rest of the Class When One Student Escalates

Managing your class when one student escalates involves conscious decision-making. A lot depends on what the class is doing when the behavior occurs. If we are gathered at Home Base or on the Learning Circle, then the impact and disruption is high. If it occurs while we are engaged with balls, tumbling mats, or other activities, then the impact on the class is lower. One of the easiest solutions is to remove the class from the vicinity of the student who is experiencing unregulated behavior and go to another part of the gym where I can continue teaching while keeping an eye on the student and the paras. These are the situations when the teamwork you and the paras have developed over time pays dividends. If we follow routines and systems, and I have clearly explained my expectations and objectives for the lesson, it's easy to stay in sync. Communication between us is second nature, and we can change and even trade roles to fit any situation. Most of the time I rely on the paras to assist individual students when their behavior escalates or when they elope. However, there are times when I want to be the one to assist, in which case I'll ask a para to temporarily take over my role as activity leader. I have different reasons for doing this, and sometimes it is because I have observed that student and para have fallen into a pattern of interaction that I want to change. I may want to try a different approach with that student.

Figuring out solutions to students' challenges is what teachers do all day long and is in a real sense what makes the job of teaching inventive and creative. However, some students come to school with issues that are very difficult for us to manage, and it can take a long time for a young teacher to fully accept that. My approach is to try to create a relationship with my students while getting the help I need from colleagues and from the adults who know my students best. The good news is that over time and with commitment, we were able to accommodate every student arriving in our school – even those whose behavior initially seemed like a constant "four alarm fire."

There are times when students' behavior escalates despite positive behavior supports you have in place. They may not have fully assimilated the concept of requesting a break in lieu of task avoidance. You may even have tried to anticipate their mood change by suggesting a break. They may simply be reacting to events or stimuli you are not aware of. Before their behavior escalates further, you may want to ask the para to take the student out of the present situation into a different environment where it might be easier for them to self-regulate. You might ask a para to try walking laps with them. Moving to a quiet corner or out into the hallway may help reduce the student's anxiety. If you feel there is no risk of the student running away, taking them outside into the fresh air is sometimes the kind of sensory break that's needed. Even if these measures do not calm your student, it certainly calms the environment for the rest of the class. If you find that going for a walk in the hallway, visiting the water fountain, standing at an open window or some other measure that is not listed on the sensory break menu is proving to be consistently effective, then you can suggest adding it to your student's BIP.

The decision to remove a student should never be taken lightly. When you remove a student, you are interrupting their access to education, and you better have a good reason, and you better have tried everything else you can think of first. An inexperienced teacher may be tempted to let the behavior continue, thinking that students with disabilities are probably somewhat used to seeing their classmates' loud and angry behavior, that it's probably not a big deal to them. I've had this exact conversation with myself. The answer I eventually came to is that students do not deserve to experience their classmate's extremely unregulated behavior along with the anxiety it can produce when there are alternatives. Not only that, but it can be embarrassing and traumatizing for the student who is struggling with their own behavior. Assisting them to an environment where they feel calmer and can regain control is the appropriate thing for a teacher to do. It is part of preserving a student's dignity. When a student is harming themselves or others or threatening to do so or when they are so loud and/or upset that teaching and learning cannot continue, it's clear that something needs to change. As the adult in loco parentis, I need to know when the threshold is reached and exceeded. However, it goes without saying that my goal is not to let behavior escalate to that point but to use my knowledge and intuition, as well as that of my colleagues, plus the student's behavior plans to calm the environment and allow teaching and learning to continue.

Maintaining Student Engagement

I have many students, some with IEPs and some without, who are not verbally communicative and have difficulty with social cues which can manifest as an unwillingness to participate. As a teacher, it can be challenging to keep students engaged with the class so that they can experience the pleasure of physical activity, so much of which involves play and cooperation with peers. Keeping students engaged demands all my effort, and allowing students to disengage because that is their tendency or because I am frustrated with the difficulty of communicating with them is not an option. When a student disengages from the class activity, opposes participation, walks away, or sits down in a corner without permission, what is your response? I try to view the behavior as I would with all my students: inappropriate avoidance of work. Unless there is a good reason for excusing a student, such as a health condition, we do not offer the option of "non-participation." I doubt very much that most parents would want us to.

Having limited verbal language need not be a barrier to interacting with peers and teachers. The half-hour twice a week I have with my students, including those with special needs, is a small fraction of the time they spend with their teacher, paras, and classmates, all of whom have more experience interacting and communicating with them than I do. I try to learn all the buddy systems and communication systems that are already in place for my student and apply them in PE. According to Koegel and LaZebnik, *Overcoming Autism* (2004), "The very defining feature of autism is communication delays...which affects all types of interactions with other people and often includes an apparent lack of interest in talking to or communicating with anyone, even Mom and Dad" (p. 99). In the chapter titled, "Ending the Long Silence: Teaching Your Child to Communicate," Koegel and LaZebnik emphasize that parents and caregivers need to prioritize connection and communication since the tendency of many children with ASD is to disengage. They argue that maintaining an environment saturated with language and interactivity from an early age is key to successful language development:

> ...if we start intervention for communication before the age of three, about 95 percent of children with autism who are *completely* (their emphasis) nonverbal will learn to communicate verbally if the right approach is used... For children starting the intervention between the ages of three and five who are nonverbal, the probability goes down a bit, to 85 to 90 percent;

When Mario leaves the track and lies down on the floor, I know it is not because I have given him an impossible or inappropriate task, and therefore I give him a specific direction such as "one more giraffe walk and one backwards walk and then you can have a water break." We never allow Esther to climb the mat stack although she would stay happily occupied if we allowed her to do that. Sometimes it surprised me how persistent the paraeducators were with students who were averse to tasks. There were times when I was tempted to give up and let them have their way – allowed them to stop participating and walk away or sit down. The paras did not put up with that. In a calm but forceful manner, they did not allow students to opt out of most activities even when they cried or ran away. On more than one occasion, Chandra and Carol told me that such and such a student had to learn that this was school, not home, and that work was not optional. As a parent or a teacher, when a child is very distressed it is hard to not give in, but if we do, we run the risk of encouraging avoidance or attention-seeking. On the other hand, the decision to offer a change of pace or sensory break usually followed a previously designed plan that included a few options for a student to choose from. These preferred activities and/or locations allowed students to calm down from feelings of anxiety, anger, or dysregulation, and return to a learning posture.

Sensory Diversity

One day Romy came to PE in an upset state. Fran, who is one of Romy's most important adults and is assigned to one-on-one support, said that she had had a difficult time leaving the

FIGURE 4.3 We have different reactions to sensory input.

classroom for PE because it meant stopping an activity she enjoyed. Nevertheless, they did a few warmup laps together and went to Home Base with the rest of the class. When Fran signaled Romy to be seated on her number, Romy became agitated. Fran took Romy's PEC cards out of her pocket and showed Romy the one she was supposed to use to request a break, but Romy pushed it away, went over to the wall, knocked down the mat that was leaning there and lay down on top of it. She began to cry and rock back and forth while trying to pull the mat over herself. Most of the items on Romy's Sensory Break Menu did not seem useful at the time, except possibly for the weighted blanket. Worried that her behavior might escalate, one of the paras jogged down to room 407 to retrieve it. In the meantime, I watched Romy carefully and noticed that she was pulling up on the edge of the mat. It seemed that she was trying to pull it across her body, so I helped her. Wrapped in the mat, she began to calm down, and while Fran stayed with her, I took the class to the mat hexagon for some steps and balances.

If we ask the question, "What did Romy's behavior *do for her*?" we can readily answer that it resulted in:

1. Interrupting what we were doing, i.e. sitting together on the floor at Home Base talking about our next activity
2. Focusing my attention as well as that of two paraeducators on Romy
3. Romy leaving the immediate instructional space
4. Altering Romy's sensory environment

Were all those responses critical to calming her, or perhaps only one or two of them? Were other things causing Romy pain that I was unaware of? One way to narrow it down would be to try the above, one at a time, the next time Romy had a behavior escalation, record the results on data sheets, and begin assembling a database.

I have had at least two students who craved the opposite sensation. They were calmed by hard impact. These were students (both happen to have been boys, and one of them did have an ADHD diagnosis) who not only couldn't stay still but habitually slid, crashed, collided, jumped, and slammed their bodies from heights whenever they could. There is a whole range of sensory preferences among students who have autism, intellectual disabilities, and various physical conditions. We all have these preferences, some to a stronger degree than others. Give me a minute to think about it, and I can probably come up with a list of my own. In addition to the swaddling and impact preferences I just mentioned, I had a student who loved to swing upside-down on the jungle gym and wouldn't stop until recess was over, at which time we practically had to pull him off the bar. A sensation that would make most people physically ill was very enjoyable to him.

Thinking in Pictures, by Temple Grandin, totally opened my eyes to the fact that some people experience the sensory world in ways that we cannot begin to imagine. If you want to put yourself in the shoes of a person with Autism Spectrum Disorder, this book is an excellent source. The chapter entitled "Sensory Problems in Autism" is an incredible journey thanks to Grandin's ability to convey her thoughts and perceptions as a person on the spectrum…:

> When I was six, I would wrap myself up in blankets and get under sofa cushions, because the pressure was relaxing. I used to daydream for hours in elementary school about constructing a device that would apply pressure to my body. I visualized a box with an inflatable liner that I could lie in. It would be like being totally encased in inflatable splints.

Like Romy, Grandin was a "pressure seeker," and it was this trait that led her eventually to designing and patenting a device that is used today by people with this type of sensory distortion. Knowing where our physical body ends and the outside world begins is central to our sense of self, but, amazingly, some people have severe boundary problems. Grandin describes one man who does not know where he is if he cannot see his legs, and a woman, Donna Williams, who has a fractured perception of her body in which she could perceive only one part at a time. Similar fracturing occurred when she looked at things around her. She could only look at one small part of an object at a time. Donna tapped rhythmically and sometimes slapped herself to determine where her body boundaries were. When her senses became overloaded with painful stimuli, she bit herself, not realizing that she was biting her own body.

Reading these passages put Romy's behavior into perspective. I no longer saw it as bizarre or illogical. Instead, I began to feel compassion for her because I imagined that she was navigating a different sensory world that must have felt painful and scary at times.

Unless you have spent a lot of time with them, you might not know how a student who has autism processes sensory input. Their important adults, friends, and family will have spent enough time with them in various environments to acquire a reasonable understanding of the sensory inputs that are disturbing or calming. If you are going to teach students who have autism, it will be advantageous to begin acquiring an understanding of your students' sensory idiosyncrasies. Why does your student run from the group, wave their arms, make loud noises, or engage in stimming behaviors when they come into your teaching space? Are there more people than they're used to during the rest of the day? Is it noisier? Do hard surfaces create a harsher acoustic environment? Are there multiple moving objects? Perhaps your gym is next to the kitchen, and the smells of food cooking pervade the space. We all notice these stimuli, but we all don't respond to them in the same way. We have an uncanny ability to filter out unimportant sounds and sights and instantaneously shift to those that are noteworthy or emergent. However, a person who has autism may have sensory issues that cause unpredictable responses. The implications for learning, attending and being able to focus on task are obvious.

What Does It Mean to "Pay Attention," and Why Is It so Complicated?

Scott Grafton's *Physical Intelligence: The Science of How the Body and the Mind Guide Each Other through Life* provides many insights into the mysteries surrounding our ability to focus attention on what is important (like the teacher's voice) and ignore other ambient inputs. The chapter, "The Space We Create," examines the concepts of vigilance and attention as they relate to the larger question of how our brains create the virtual operational space that surrounds us – the volume of space immediately around us and beyond that we can picture in our mind's eye. You lie in bed at night, and you hear the clothes dryer buzzer, the German Shepherd on the hill behind your house, the neighbor's garage door, the sound of the wind blowing through the tall firs, and you can "see" each of them. But what if, mixed in with those, was the sound of the knob on your front door slowly turning? That would jump to the forefront of your awareness and eclipse all the other sounds. Grafton describes the human ability to selectively attend:

> There is magic in this ability to control whatever bits of space we want to attend to: they can be shrunk, stretched, or shoved to the side...The metaphor for what the brain is doing in this case is the zoom lens. Its job is to search through space to find something specific and, once found, to focus on the target...The flip side is a form of attention needed to filter out unwanted information. A person strolling down Fifth Avenue in Manhattan is bombarded by both the press of pedestrians and bright, shining objects in store windows. Imagine if you were unable to ignore all the window displays on Fifth Avenue. You wouldn't be much better than an excited puppy, running from item to item. And yet, a person talking on her cell phone to a lover is able to pass by all of it, oblivious to the visual clutter. The capacity to filter selectively different sensations that are being dutifully recorded by our eyes and ears is an extraordinary evolutionary accomplishment. At the same time, there needs to be sufficient leakiness in this filtering operation so that conspicuous events or noteworthy objects can be noticed.

As I sit at my computer, I picture the path that my students take as they walk down the carpeted hall to the gym entrance. When they arrive at the gym doors, they pass into a small vestibule, turn left, and enter an enormous space: the ceiling is three times higher than anywhere else in the school, the space is wide open, there is no furniture, no nooks, no private space, and the auditory environment changes suddenly. As Grafton points out, a lot of human evolution has gone into creating our ability to make sense of sensory input so that most of us agree on what is happening around us. But what if my sensory schematic does not tell me the same thing it tells you? My point is that we think of "attention" as a simple, straightforward skill analogous to aiming an antenna at a radio signal, but, as Grafton points out, it is anything but. When our students appear not to notice the obvious attention target – THE TEACHER! – and instead stare at your collection of college pennants or become anxious, you might consider that as a reason to investigate your classroom's visual and auditory features to see if you can make changes that calm your students and result in fewer distractions.

Is attention a single variable like loudness or brightness, or is it composed of multiple variables? After years of teaching and waging a constant struggle to gain and keep my students' attention, I've come to think of it not so much as a "thing" they need to have or acquire or dial up, like the volume on a radio. Now, I tend to think of attention more like a sixth sense. It's always there, and one can turn it to different targets, focus it or filter it. We all have our susceptibilities. My aunt used to "bathe" in Tea Rose perfume. Now if I'm on a bus or plane when someone is wearing that cloying scent, it completely dominates my attention and renders me incapable of concentrating on a book or on my thoughts. As Scott Grafton points out in *Physical Intelligence*, our attention to the surrounding world must be porous enough to admit critical information when it arises suddenly and impervious enough to allow us to focus on what we care about in the moment. The lesson for teachers is that getting our students' attention and engagement is going to involve a lot more than just talking loudly. There are several things to consider, including

- Sensory diversity from individual to individual
- Reducing distractions in the environment
- Instruction that proceeds logically and takes students' knowledge and background into account

Every new school year I have a ritual of walking around the building and looking in all the classrooms to see how teachers set up their rooms. The variety is stunning. There are those teachers who clearly don't pay much attention to ambience or lighting and aren't bothered by over-stimulating clutter. If I were a student in one of those rooms, you could automatically drop my grade average 25 percent due to environmental discomfort. Then there are those teachers who are amazingly thoughtful about the way they arrange furniture, and use multiple lighting sources and wall textures in ways that create privacy space, small group space, contemplative space, coziness, and tranquility. Lighting should be a paramount consideration in any workspace. I have never given it much thought, but I realize that I often adjust the lighting panel in the gym depending on the activity, on my mood, and on how I want to influence class behavior. Also, for someone who is easily distracted, like me, placing and hanging more posters, books, supplies, and knickknacks on counters, walls, ceilings, and in front of windows than is necessary for current reference and learning will only provide endless opportunities for students to focus on what is not important, and can even create unsettling emotions and real discomfort. The senses need to be able to rest and selectively focus so that the really important work inside your own head can happen without distractions.

I try to get answers to questions about sensory issues and the stimuli that adversely affect students the same way I do with other unknowns. I talk to those who know my students best and learn everything I can from them. I use those tips to begin making incremental changes. Like trying to figure out what foods you might be allergic to, you don't learn anything definitive if you change a bunch of variables at once. Try one change and see if it makes a difference. For example, it didn't take long to discover that Kayden was a calmer young man when he was working alone with Dawn. I also found that lyrical, upbeat tunes like "My Favorite Things" or Jimmy Cliff's "I Can See Clearly Now" seem to put my students at ease. It was also clear that all my Fireflies had limited patience with direct instruction.

In an earlier chapter I talked about "Lydia" and the importance of music and sound. She was a student who depended on visual and hearing perception due to her mobility issues. The lesson here is not that pressure or swaddling are techniques that you should have in your "sensory toolkit." The lesson is that close observation and critical reflection are indispensable qualities in a teacher. You will start to notice behaviors that may have a pattern which could lead you to responses that you can generalize. If you are not regularly taking the time to devote your attention to observation, or even worse, you watch but don't set aside time to reflect on what you are seeing and hearing, then the train has left the station, and you've missed it.

Staying Focused When There Are so Many Distractions: Ramp up Your Learning Prompts

Keeping attention focused is a constant challenge. One of the indicators that a student will be successful in groupwork and when they are included in a gen. ed. class is the ability to pay attention to instruction and pay attention to classmates. It is that ability that influenced the decision to include Grant and Nanda in gen. ed. PE. Mario and Nolan are included at times but require one-on-one adult support to guide them and help adapt activities. Nolan is an interesting boy. He so clearly enjoys PE. He's got a great smile. He laughs, he verbalizes, he reaches for others and walks to wherever there is the most commotion. Nolan is only interested in a piece of equipment if someone else is playing with it. And, if another student is acting silly, like Esther escaping the office with an armful of jump ropes, Nolan finds that particularly entertaining and will pay attention to nothing else. I cannot capture his attention if there is any other action occurring within sight. Our only recourse is to use stronger prompts such as reconfiguring the environment around him to block his view of other students. The paras sometimes do this by standing between him and the others or by taking him to a corner of the gym. We even use mats stood on edge to create a private space for him. But even this won't work if he hears commotion nearby. He just stops what he's doing and heads for it.

I can recall a game we played as part of our tossing/basketball unit. We placed plastic tubs against the wall for targets. Each tub had a different type of ball or tossing object. To discourage students from standing too close to the tub, we placed carpet squares at a distance to mark where to stand. In their enthusiasm to hit the targets students tended to ignore the spots and move closer, so I replaced the spots with folded mats that they had to stand on, and that solved the problem. I would call that a "stronger learning prompt." We ran the activity as a station rotation so that after a minute or two everyone rotated and experienced a different throwing object (yarn ball, rubber animal, wiffleball, gator skin ball, etc.) It didn't matter what station Nolan was at. He wouldn't stop turning to watch his neighbors. I stood mats up on either side of his station creating his own private court, and that didn't work. After one or two tosses he

FIGURE 4.4 Configure equipment and create an environment that focuses attention on the task.

peeked around the side of the mat to watch Nanda. I don't think of Nolan as a student who has no attention span or lacks ability to attend. Rather, I think of him as someone who has "stubborn attention" that is difficult to re-direct. That characterization shifts the concept from "deficit" to "difference." Either way, it makes it difficult for Nolan to be successfully included in gen. ed. PE. To create the conditions where I can capture his attention and direct it so that he can practice the skills he needs, the best option is to pull him aside for one-on-one instruction away from the rest of the class or even at another time so that he has a chance to learn and practice the appropriate skills.

The most challenging time to maintain our class's attention and direct their focus, whether it is a class of students with special needs or a class of neurotypical kids, is during seat time when I need to discuss academic content, safety, or just take care of administrative business. I find that is where 90 percent of the off-task disruptive behavior occurs. Sometimes no matter how great your diagrams are and how much you try to turn up the enthusiasm voltage, kids don't want to sit on their butts in PE. For students who have communication deficits it's difficult to know exactly which aspect of direct instruction is most tiresome to them. It could be what they perceive as the teacher's prolonged intrusion into their space, or the stream of verbal commands and direct eye contact. One of our most important tools is the habit of monitoring our students while instructing. We watch for signs of engagement: eye contact, body language and fidgeting, side conversations, and compliance with instructions. The habit of *self*-monitoring is also important. How long have I been talking/monologuing while they have been sitting as a captive audience? I have an internal clock that warns me when I've been talking for more than five minutes. Even though the information may be important, is it really necessary at the moment? Can I deliver it at another time or while my students are active? I remind myself that we have only have 30 minutes for everything: warmup, instruction, demonstration, practice, activity, wrap-up, cleanup, and lineup.

Students can acquire academic content while moving. For example, students assimilate academic content on nutrition when we play chase and flee games that simulate the inter-relation between calorie intake, physical activity, and body composition. I think of a game like Calorie Burner (described in the chapter on fitness activities) that simulates the balancing act between calories consumed and calories burned as an example of a contextual learning prompt. Information that students are resistant to in a direct instruction setting becomes more accessible when acted out with movement in response to pictures of food. That is a strong and effective learning prompt.

Teachers know that a disorganized lesson that does not lead students from what they know to what they need to learn in a clear, methodical way is not likely to build confident learners and is more likely to cause disengagement. I am reminded of times when I was a student in class and suddenly felt lost. For my students with autism, sensory differences, or intellectual disabilities I can't imagine how that phenomenon translates to their experience.

Positive Behavior Support

Adapted Physical Education (Block 2016) contains a chapter, "Positive Behavior Support of Children with Challenging Behaviors." Block describes how Positive Behavior Support can help to put challenging and seemingly random behavior into a systematic context that makes a proactive approach possible. A traditional management approach might try to eliminate unwanted behavior with negative consequences and react to positive behavior with rewards without concern for why the behavior occurred. PBS emphasizes prevention by teaching students more appropriate alternative behaviors and supporting the student through systematic planning rather than trial and error. The following are some of the key elements of the PBS approach:

- ♦ Measure frequency and duration to help identify unwanted behaviors.
- ♦ Examine the antecedents/causes of the behavior.

- Analyze the Who, What, When, Where of the behavior.
- Develop a Functional Behavior Assessment.
- Prevent behavior by establishing class rules and enforcing them.
- Know students' preferences and preferred activities.
- Teach social and self-management skills.
- A well-designed lesson can provide intrinsic reinforcement.
- Include lessons and games that reward positive, respectful behavior.

Measuring the frequency or duration of unwanted behavior is key to identifying and isolating it from other behaviors that may not be as concerning. I use tally mark records for frequency and a stopwatch for duration. Then I transfer the results to a record book that summarizes the data by student for every PE class. When the behavior occurs, who is present, when and where does it occur, and what is usually happening when it does? Having different adults chart these observations is important. At times I want a para to observe and record while I'm teaching, but we also switch roles so that I can observe behavior with particular attention to interactions between students and paras. When principals come into the gym to observe as part of my evaluation, they often ask if there is anything specific I want them to watch for. I might describe the target behavior we have identified and ask them to record frequency and duration.

Many factors come into play when trying to prevent unwanted behaviors. Am I familiar with my **students' preferences and preferred activities**? When strategically inserted into my lesson plan, they motivate students. Knowing my students' emotional state on a given day is very helpful. There is a **"Tap your feelings" board** posted on the wall at the entrance to our gym with faces portraying different emotions – happy, sad, fearful, tired, ill, bored. I stand nearby as students tap it. It is a quick way for students to communicate their feelings to me, and that has helped to avoid conflicts and keep things positive. Some students are better able to maintain learning posture when they can bring a **special toy** or fidget object or when they can get a certain colored ball or scarf from the PE supplies. Do your students know and understand your **classroom rules**, and do you enforce them? How can I expect appropriate, on-task behavior if my students are not clear on what that means? Virtually all teachers post lists of rules, but if they are not accompanied by clear visuals, some students will not access them. We use consistent language and gestures when we remind students of the rules, and, when possible, we touch a visual representation simultaneously. "Hands to self." "Eyes on teacher."

My goal is to create a **well-designed lesson** that keeps students intrinsically motivated. That does not happen every day, but there are tools that increase the odds. **Instruction that proceeds logically** and builds skill upon skill results in students feeling empowered. When **games and activities reward positive behavior** and respectful peer interaction, frustration and conflict are reduced, and we create the conditions where students take responsibility for their own learning.

Think about It Questions

When you hear the phrase, "the teacher–student relationship," what do you think of? Are these amorphous feelings and thoughts or do they have a specific form? What do you think can be gained by defining the phrase for yourself?

Did you ever find yourself having to "fight your way through your own negative impressions [of a student] in order to connect with the learner within?" Did you tell anyone else about it? Did you get help from a colleague, friend, or spouse? Describe that process.

If you had a student who had an Individualized Education Program (IEP), and they were exhibiting extreme distress by yelling and crying, would you try to comfort them just as you would any other student? Would you approach them differently? If so, explain.

Assume that negative behavior is either about getting something (attention, sensory stimulation, status, rewards, power) or avoiding something (pain, boredom, anxiety, fear, someone

Understanding Behavior, Sensory Diversity, and Challenges to Engagement ◆ 89

not liked). Start a behavior chart. Include columns for student names, concerning behaviors, possible cause getting/avoiding. Share results with colleagues whose charts include some of the same students.

Can you identify the *who, what, when, where* when disengagement and unexpected behavior occur most frequently? Reflect on your strategies for maintaining student engagement. Who are the coworkers who might observe you teach and assist you in identifying potential issues and solutions?

Does your school or organization have systems in place for dealing with difficult events, so you are not having to figure out what to do every time as though it were a brand-new problem? Think of an instance like Kayden's acting out or an uncomfortable interaction with a student. Copy and fill out the "Student Incident Reflection Tool."

Add to this list of students' behavior triggers:
◆ not getting what they want
◆ having to stop doing something that they like
◆ having to leave a place where they are comfortable
◆ having to work when they don't feel like it
◆ missing home
◆ wanting mom or dad
◆ not feeling well
◆ ____
◆ ____
◆ ____

Do this activity with a trusted partner in case difficult emotions arise. In the chapter, you read an example of a panic sensation induced by an illusion. With a partner, try to put yourself in the shoes of someone whose fear or panic reaction did not have a recognizable cause. Have you ever had an equivalent experience?

Whether a student is gifted and talented or has learning disabilities, conferencing with parents can involve sharing knowledge about areas where they are falling short of expectations as well as their wonderful qualities and achievements. Imagine a phone call with Romy's parents after the incident when she became very agitated, and you tried calming her with the gym mat. You are prepared with a list of positives and negatives.

Notes

1 NCTSN Populations at Risk > Intellectual and Developmental Disabilities.
2 Dewey, John (1938) *Experience & Education*. Collier Books.
3 One of the most valuable professional development meetings we had at school was a panel of school parents who were from various countries. They talked about the education systems that they had grown up in, what they expected to find in the US, and how what their children were experiencing in school differed from their expectations.
4 The Right Response Workshop is a program of the Service Alternatives Training Institute, a Division of Service Alternatives, Inc.

5
Incremental Steps to Learning

Authenticity, Dependability and Trust

When I turned nineteen, I got a job as a counselor in a summer camp in upstate New York. Its mission was to provide a classic "sleepaway" camp experience for boys and girls with diverse needs and abilities. The camp directors tried to prepare us by giving us a course in psychology before the campers arrived. Every day for a week we gathered in the mess hall and attended a class taught by a psych professor. I don't remember much about the class, but I clearly remember the gist of his final message to us, and when I heard it, I thought to myself, "Okay, I can do that." He emphasized that we were not there to cure, counsel, or provide therapy.

Our job was to approach our campers no differently than we would any 9- or 10-year-old in our care: Be responsible to them, keep them safe, pay attention to them, be a big brother, be a shoulder to lean on, have fun, and learn. The message was: Be our best selves, and be authentic. Having chosen a career in teaching, that message holds a lot of truth for me. It contains an affirmation that I am worthy and have something positive to contribute to my students beyond academics. My willingness to be myself with students communicates my trust in them and invites their trust in return. In being authentic, I am communicating dependability and predictability. This is the context in which

I try to find ways of getting to know my students so that I can be a more effective teacher.

Consistent Routine: The Warmup

> **Cumulative mastery** of the critical elements is the key to a maturing pattern of skill development by the end of elementary school physical education. Depth of learning experiences with focused practice provides the maturing skill pattern.
>
> (Couturier et al., 2014)

Building on a foundation of trust and positive regard, teaching students with disabilities and special needs proceeds gradually and methodically. It can take much more time for them to acquire skills. More practice and repetition are required. The warmup track is a very good platform for skill building, and students generally prefer a locomotor activity to staying in one place. There

FIGURE 5.1 Multiple pieces of equipment are added to the warmup track to offer a variety of locomotor challenges.

are endless possibilities for modifications: size, shape, surface, duration, intensity, equipment, travel modes, individual or small group. I generally change one feature at a time to maintain continuity and avoid negative reactions to unexpected stimuli. The warmup track is always the first activity for all students upon entering the gym. With their pent-up energy, students tend to bolt for it as soon as they come through the doors. The setup I use with gen. ed. classes consists simply of four cones arranged in a large rectangle, but to adapt it for all students involves adding stronger environmental prompts that reinforce the path and build in more locomotor options. Many kinds of equipment suffice for the purpose, but I find that a combination of poly spots, step boxes, and Bosu[1] balls strike just the right balance. The poly spots are trail markers that make the path clearer, and the step boxes and Bosu balls add an important third dimension. This equipment is low profile so students can maintain speed, but it offers them different options for modes of travel: tiptoe, leap, bounce, and hop. With care, students can negotiate the track forwards, sideways, and backwards. Students who tend to elope when the track lacks these extra features remain in the instructional space longer. Usually, two or three paraeducators accompany the Firefly class, and we start walking in a counterclockwise direction. The paras stick with the students they are assigned due to their higher needs, assisting in the performance of tasks that I assign and model. If I want students to practice travel modes and follow my model, I prepare the track without extra equipment. We do about two laps for each movement, and from walking we transition to jogging, side slides, chicken walk, eagle, monkey, backwards and giraffe, as well as any kind of cardio and muscle endurance exercise I can disguise as an animal. If you came into our gym at this point, here is what you might find:

First, you would hear a jazz tune or standard playing through my PA system. Two boys and a girl walk around the cones, hands in the air imitating a giraffe. Another student strolls with a para by her side and encouraging her, "Giraffe walk, arms in the air!," while lifting the student's arms. Another student accompanied by a para walks and skips and repeats a phrase I don't quite understand. The para is content for her just to keep that pace.

One of the two boys drops his hands and walks over to the wall where he sits down. I jog over and encourage him to stand up. I tell him we have a few more things to do and then scooters. "Scooters," he announces.

"Giraffe walk first."

"Scooters."

"Giraffe walk first, then scooters.[2] Stand up Mario. "Come with me – let's go to the whiteboard and look at the schedule." At eye level, the agenda was easy to see, and students can touch the words:

- Warmup Laps
- Learning Circle
- Toss and Catch
- Scooters
- Cleanup

A bright red magnet was stuck to the board next to "Warmup Laps." I touched the magnet and asked, "Mario, what are we doing now?"

"Warmup laps."

"What comes next?" I pointed to the learning circle and then to each agenda item successively as Mario answered each question appropriately. We went back to the track and walked together.

Kayden is smiling and traveling with a walk-skip step. Dawn walks by his side. I notice that if she goes more than six feet away from him, to help another student, Kayden's demeanor changes, and he turns to watch her. I have the sense that he's feeling a little unsteady, a little vulnerable. When she returns to his side, he resumes his skip and arm swinging. The other boy is Grant. He has stopped being a giraffe and is running hard around the cones. "Go Grant, go!" I cheer.

Esther has disappeared into my office. I know what she's doing from the sounds emanating: pulling all the jump ropes off the rolling rack. I jog into the office and escort her out. "Oh Esther! You're not allowed in the office. Come on, I have something for you outside." Esther races out ahead of me straight for the big whiteboard and starts rubbing out today's agenda. Kayden is still doing well, Mario is lying down on the floor now, and Grant has stopped running. One para pursues Esther and is pretty angry with her for erasing the board. About five minutes is our limit on the warmup track. Because it is such an important exercise and learning platform for all students, I assess for elopement behavior using a simple tally mark system.

Direct Instruction: The Learning Circle

It's time to switch gears. "Learning circle everybody!" I call out. The paras all repeat "Learning circle!" The **Learning Circle**, a twelve-foot diameter circle in the center of the gym, is my preferred gathering and instruction location. In the learning circle, I can face the students, and they can face me, and being concentrically located in the center of the track, there is an easy transition from warmup laps to non-locomotor activity. Poly spot markers or carpet squares are important environmental cues which mark exact locations on the circle for each student so that little descriptive language or explanation is necessary to tell the students where to go. I am on a spot too because I am modeling my expectations. However, because their job is to facilitate and maintain each activity's expectations, the paras usually do not have their own spots. While the students are expected to remain in place, the paras need to be mobile with their attention focused on the students, helping them to attain the correct posture for their body and for handling any equipment. This is where much of our non-locomotor direct instruction takes place, such as weight training, stretching, and balancing. Some of the pieces of equipment that we typically use on the learning circle are resistance tubes, playground balls, medicine balls, scarves, basketballs, and step boxes. I have pre-positioned half a dozen poly spots on the circle. Grant goes to one and stands on it. Nanda wants purple, but Grant has already taken the only one. "No problem, Nanda. Go over to the bucket and get purple." She busies herself with that job as we all gradually assemble on the poly spots.

I want the students' attention to be on me, not on the paras. I want their eyes and ears when I model a task. One of the most common phrases you hear paras say is, **"Eyes on teacher!"** This is a constant refrain and a very important principle in any class where instructional support staff (paraeducators, instructional coaches, physical therapists, or translators) are present. The teacher plans the lessons, organizes the content, prepares and manages the environment, delivers instruction, and models behavior. They give students appropriate feedback based on their knowledge of the students and of where the lesson is going next. If a student gets in the habit of focusing too much on their support adult or buddy during instruction, they are reinforcing dependence instead of developing appropriate learning behaviors. I won't say that it is easy to keep attention on the teacher while another adult is in your space whispering and prompting. How to help a student while they focus on the teacher is part of the skill of a good instructional support professional. If we are practicing muscle exercises with resistance tubes, and the student needs help, the para is there to model the grip or reinforce the student's grip with their own hand and to physically adjust their posture while their eyes and ears remain on me. As soon as they stop focusing on me, students invariably lose correct posture and go off task.

A tub of assorted balls is at my feet, and I call students by name to come over and select one. This stage of the lesson may seem perfunctory, but it is not. I must think about my students' individual needs for this to go well. Mario is a big boy, and since I don't have enough four-pounders for everyone, I'll make sure he gets a six-pound ball. Nolan has trouble gripping with his hands and holding much weight. I will probably give him a rubber playground ball instead of a medicine ball. Gemma always has a favorite fidget toy in her hand and often doesn't focus on instruction, but I may try her with a scarf instead of a ball because I know she likes fabrics. Kayden watches everything that goes on. I'll give him a four-pound ball. He may avoid gripping it, but I would like him to hold some weight as a kind of reminder that it's there and he needs to pay attention to it. This internal decision-making process continues through each step in the lesson and is probably one reason that teaching students who have special needs can be mentally tiring.

The students mirror my movements in exercises that develop ball-handling skill and muscle endurance with enough repetitions to reinforce patterns:

- Hold ball with two hands
- Raise above head, lower to stomach, to knees, to floor,
- Rainbow arcs
- Mini tosses
- Bounce in place

We differentiate students' expectations as some are right on point, while others lag or lose interest. Adults cue with reinforcing language that praises persistence and delineates finite pauses for rest. Holding and gripping balls was very difficult for Patrick, and catching, throwing, or bouncing was beyond his ability. I adapted for him by replacing a ball with a scarf. They were light, could be held between fingers, and tucked into clothing and shoelaces. Scarves instantly made bending, stretching, running, and dancing more fun, and from there we transitioned to tossing, floating, and catching. To add some heft and liveliness I tried weighting scarves by tying balls inside. Results were mixed, and success was sometimes short-lived, but these experiments always illuminated new possibilities. I found that my other students wanted scarves too, and rather than cause disappointment, I gave everyone scarves, so that Patrick did not stand out.

Communication Clarity and Total Physical Response

To get the behavior I want, I often must communicate with great specificity. Once students have their equipment, it's hard for them to resist playing with it. Therefore, if I want them to hold their ball or scarf, go to a location, and wait for my instructions, telling them to "go back to your spot and wait for instructions" will likely result in several students going off task and playing on their own. However, if I say, "Hold your ball between your

FIGURE 5.2 A student uses the communication poster to request a break.

knees as you walk to your spot, and when you get there, hold it under your chin," there will be a lot of laughter and enthusiasm and they're more likely to follow instructions.

If deficits in social interaction are the hallmark of autism, it follows that practicing communication is something we must work on in class. It is unavoidable. Many students have come to class with iPads loaded with communication software that utilizes photos and graphics, The technology is handy, but it is not a replacement for working on verbal and other technology-free methods of communication. For a student who does not respond to anything less than a combination of prompts, including physical, I try not to waste time with insufficient prompts that allow them to experience multiple failures. Some students go to the large vocabulary picture chart on the gym wall and converse by talking, gesturing, sign language, and/or pointing to pictures. A few students were unable to use the chart or picture cards or software technology. Though Patrick was nonverbal, as diagnosed by our school's SLP, he was a clear communicator when it came to expressing his wishes and feelings. He used physical movement (walking or grasping one's hand) and facial movement (gaze and smile) to indicate that he either wanted or did not want something. He communicated his preferences physically by heading toward the things he wanted. His vocalizations told me that he wanted something. He clearly communicated disinterest when he dropped an object or simply walked away. If he wanted to go somewhere with you, he held onto your hand

and took you in that direction or might push you to the location. In these ways, Patrick advocated for himself, and unlike some of my other students who were more limited in their ability to communicate, Patrick rarely resorted to escalated behavior, and his interactions with others tended to be friendly and calm.

One common way of getting students to respond is by offering equipment size or color choices. Not only is it important for teachers to immediately reinforce a student's appropriate use of language by, in this case, offering the red or blue ball to them when they say a color, but different teachers that the student encounters should agree on what is an acceptable pronunciation. If the initial consonant sound in "red" is enough for the PE teacher to honor the request while the classroom teacher requires the student to produce the final "D" consonant, the result might be confusion and frustration for the student. When Patrick entered the gym, he wanted to immediately join the other students who were already on the track, but Chandra made sure he went to the schedule board first and touched the track diagram icon as the other students had done. Many situations utilized a similar approach by requiring students to first make a sound or to touch the visual vocabulary chart on the wall to ask permission, make a request, or go to a location.

Before we begin **follow the leader** on the learning circle, I tell the Fireflies to stand and hug their ball as I am doing. After each command I wait for compliance before giving the next one. I want to show them how to handle their ball one-handed, two-handed, overhead, between the legs. If you want to be sure that students understand what to do and can do it, you must isolate the behavior and model it, and *only* it, until the student performs it correctly. If a PE teacher models a sequence of movements or an extraneous movement along with the desired one, they are more likely to confuse their students. They may be uncertain which of the tasks is most important, and consequently will rush through the sequence, not doing a great job on any one of them. I want everyone focused and in learning posture. That means feet on the poly spot, body and head facing me, ball in two hands. If I try to start instruction before my students are in posture, it is a guaranteed waste of time. I stand still, modelling the posture. I am silent, eyes searching them. I do not move, gesture, or speak. I am purposely reducing all their input to exactly what I want them to see, to hear and to do, with no extraneous stimuli. Whether I am teaching neurotypical students or students who have disabilities, I do not "chatter" when I'm engaged in direct instruction because the chatter can only distract, as it serves no purpose other than for me to enjoy the sound of my own voice.

TPR (Total Physical Response) is a technique used with beginners in ELL or foreign language instruction. In TPR, the teacher looks for a specific response from the student which indicates comprehension of a verbal command, such as "Donna, point to the clock." If Donna points to the clock on the wall, there is no doubt that she has understood what the teacher said. The technique isolates the skill of oral language comprehension and doesn't require the student to produce any language. Hence the name Total Physical Response. With precise substitutions, the teacher can practice selected vocabulary with the student, and having established that Donna knows what "clock" means, the teacher can substitute a phrase like, "Where is…" I intentionally use commands that prepare students for upcoming activities and any new vocabulary associated. Precision is equally important when asking questions. I avoid "yes/no" and vague questions. Yes/no questions have a built-in 50% handicap, and vague questions result in answers that don't really tell me anything. What is the point of asking, for example, "Everybody ready?" You will get an answer that proves nothing. But, if instead you say, "Everybody smile!" you'll have a pretty good idea who is following you. I might ask,

"Mario, what color is your ball?"
"Nanda, what color is Grant's ball?"
"Who has a ball with the number four?"

If we were not doing direct instruction on the learning circle, the **Mat Circle** was usually station two. A variant of the learning circle, the mat circle was a hexagon arrangement of six folded gym mats where students practiced TPR and singing, step-ups, balances, and ball-passing games. It was an ideal place to cool down after warmups, focus on each other and begin talking. TPR usually consisted of simple commands and responses that encouraged interaction:

- Wave to/Say Good Morning to (name)
- Point to the teacher/Point to (para's name)
- Point to station 1/station 3
- Point to the climbing wall/(specific equipment in that day's setup)

Because **action songs** were practiced in their classroom and were familiar to students, they were almost always part of the mat circle routine in PE, and a student was always asked to pick one. "Head, Shoulders, Knees and Toes," "Itsy Bitsy Spider," and "Hokie Pokie" were our favorites. Any song or game, like Rock, Paper, Scissors, which practiced language, repetition, movement, and coordination was ideal for students with diverse disabilities. Key look-fors were based on a range of participation behaviors, and I assessed using a simple chart and tally marks:

- Student faces the group.
- Student has eyes on teacher or singers.
- Student mouths/sings some words.
- Student uses motion and body part at appropriate times.

As a qualified physical education teacher, it would be completely understandable to wonder, "Here I am with all my training, coursework, advanced degrees and experience singing 'The Itsy Bitsy Spider.' Is this really what I'm getting paid for?" The answer is absolutely, emphatically *YES*…and with energy, enthusiasm, and good humor! The only questions one really needs to ask are whether the activity is consistent with one's goals for the students and whether it is effective, assessable, and enjoyable.

There are many good reasons for paring down your speech to the essentials when you are teaching. 1. You probably have English Language Learners (ELLs) in your class for whom idiomatic chatter is impossible to decipher. **2**. You will have one or two students with attention deficit disorder (ADD) or a case of goofiness who will end up focusing on your asides and witticisms rather than the instructional content – that is, if they are not already focused on the squeaking noise their shoe sole is making. 3. Some of your students are not auditory learners. Their strength is in visual or hands-on learning, in which case their learning won't kick in until you provide for that. A PE teacher who rattles on and forces their students to sit for what seems to them like an eternity is going to lose a third of their class's attention after five minutes. 4. Economy and specificity of language forces you, the teacher, to be certain of your purpose and process.

I Learn a Lesson and a Different Way to Communicate

About five years ago, we had an autism behavior consultant at school off and on for much of the year. He was not a school district employee, but an independent contractor hired to come in and work with specific students on specific issues. He was a person that you noticed. He had a big, but quiet presence. He didn't seem to invite casual conversation with staff and appeared to be very much "all business." There was a little bit of mystery about him. It was as if he spoke a different dialect than the rest of us (although I later found out he grew up in Texas.) When he used certain words, they often didn't mean what I took them to mean, and he talked in short, sparse sentences that, frankly, left me scratching my head. But there was no doubt that Ed had a way with autistic children. I often saw him standing with the room 407 class and paras in hallways, in doorways, at the top of stairs. He was always modelling how to interact with students, and he would use his body in a very intentional way to create space, reduce space and even squeeze space. Granted, he was a big man, and his size and gender (our staff is over 90% female) were enough for people to take notice. However, the techniques he demonstrated worked almost as well when other staff used them. I watched him closely whenever I had the opportunity. Students that were in mid meltdown would usually grow calm when Ed stood next to them. Amazingly, I don't think I ever saw him touch a student. He just had a way of standing, turning, walking, and using his hands that communicated something very clear to students.

Occasionally, he accompanied the Fireflies to PE where his assignment was to work with Kayden and with whichever para was supporting him. It was during those sessions that I gained insight into "non-invasive," non-contact means of maneuvering students using only my body position and presence. I remember one particular mini lesson that Ed gave me. He had been watching me trying to get Kayden to stand up and follow me to the door. I had walked up to him and told him to follow me, but Kayden wouldn't move. I started taking steps and waving my arms trying to get him to move, and it was having no effect. Ed stood up from his chair near the wall where he had been watching and walked over.

"You're confusing him."

"Really?"

"You're giving him multiple directions, and he's not used to that."

"I'm just telling him to follow me."

"He's not in posture."

"What do you mean, 'posture'?"

"He's not in posture. He's sitting down. He's right. You're wrong. He's where she (he pointed to Dawn) told him to be."

"So, what do I do?"

"He's got to stand up first. You have to get him into posture."

I'm still confused by his use of the word, 'posture.' Is he supposed to stand up straighter or lean forward?

"He's got to stand up. Get him into posture!"

"Uh huh. Okay. Kayden, stand up." I looked at him and gave him the sign language gesture for standing – two fingers standing on up-turned palm. He stood up. "Good Kayden, thank you!" It's time for the second direction. "Kayden, follow me," and I turned halfway around and started to walk toward the door. Kayden did not move. Ed seemed to be enjoying this. I walked back. Kayden looked at Ed. Having received eye contact, Ed said to Kayden, "Walk, Kayden," and as he did so, he extended his arm in the direction of the door and slowly started to move. As Kayden began to move with him, Ed continued toward the door, arm still extended, forming a kind of corridor between himself and the wall, down which Kayden walked.

I learned a few things in that lesson. With some students I need to break directions down into one step commands. My body language needs to mirror my words accurately. Finally, I learned that being "in posture" included several elements, in addition to stance, that indicate readiness to attend.

Eye Contact: Toss and Catch, Moving to the Ball

Romy normally did not sustain eye contact, although she had no difficulty tracking me if we were playing catch or dribbling a ball together. She did not focus much on her classmates either or try to engage them in play. When she and I tossed a ball back and forth, her gaze was always to the side toward some distant spot. She did not look at me or at the ball until it was almost upon her. Then she would give it a quick glance, just long enough to catch it, but when she tossed it back to me her eyes were already elsewhere. We depend so much on eye contact to maintain interpersonal connection. A person's expression and, particularly their eyes, give me permission, in a sense, to continue doing whatever it is we're doing. Turning away is a sure signal of disinterest. However, these rules are altered with persons who have ASD, and, as the adult, I must recognize that and look for other ways that my students signal their attention and interest. A basic principle is that as long as Romy or Aaron or Kayden continued to engage in an activity like tossing, rolling, or skipping, I could assume that the activity had value.

Let's say that my student is doing very well on a task like playing catch. They are making accurate tosses and solid catches. If I'm having trouble making up my mind whether to continue or alter the activity, I review what my goals are with the student. It might be time to change if we are starting a basketball unit because there are a few other skills to learn and practice. If my student has had a difficult day prior to PE and took a long time to focus, then I am more likely to continue the toss and catch routine. If they had been upset and were showing discomfort, the repetition is calming. We don't stop riding a bicycle or hitting a tennis ball against a wall once we've proved to ourselves that we can do it. Repetition feels good. It focuses your mind and relaxes you at the same time. I will watch for signs that my student's anxiety is lessening, which might be accompanied by a decrease in stimming behavior.

If you let your own internal clock tell you when to stop an activity, you may not be allowing your students the practice they need. Your inner voice may be telling you, "That's enough time spent on that; it's boring now; time to do the next thing." But that is *your* point of view. What do your students experience? All the people in school who know the students in 407 best have told me that their students need much more repetition than other students and that it is totally okay to extend activities longer than I normally would.

Whether the drill is soccer or basketball or fielding baseballs, the player needs to learn that the ball rarely comes straight to them. Anticipating the trajectory and moving your body into position to get the ball is a key skill, so I tried to work on that with Romy by passing the ball incrementally farther to her left and to her right so that she had to reach for it. If she could reach it without taking a step, she was okay, but motivating her to move her feet to the ball was very difficult. If the ball went past her, she didn't turn to watch it but would tend to start repetitive vocal patterns and hand flapping. Sometimes we had more success working in a corner of the gym where the ball would rebound off the walls and not escape. Even when the ball returned close to her, it took some time and encouragement for Romy to bend down and pick it up. Like many of my students with disabilities, Romy's skills were limited by her ability to focus her attention on the task. When she was no longer interested in pursuing an activity, I learned that it was best not to push it and to always be prepared to move onto something else. However, we also discovered activities and environments where Romy was able to focus her attention well.

Small Motor Activities to Practice Visual Attention: Stack Cups

The prevalence of motor impairments at a young age, often before social or communicative impairments are apparent, suggests that motor characteristics may be a core feature of autism (Fournier, Hass, Naik, Lodha, & Cauraugh, 2010 as cited in Block 2016, p. 191). Improving eye focus and visual tracking improves motor skills, coordination, and reaction time. Small motor activities are a very good way to challenge students to work on visual focus. For a student like Romy, who tends to gaze at the background and who likes to keep walking, why not make it easier by reducing the distractions and reducing the space? There are small motor activities that we can do in the classroom sitting at tables with the equipment within arm's reach. My students are accustomed to working at their seats and know what "feet on floor and hands in lap" means. One of our favorite activities is stack cups. Our school invested in the Speed Stacks "Sport Pack," which contains a large quantity of cups divided into colored and patterned sets. I was able to persuade our principal to purchase it with building funds instead of using my budget since it could serve the entire school when weather or other events prevented outdoor recess. There is an endless variety of things you can do with stack cups or with any small sortable, stackable, nest-able items. While stack cups have become very popular as a competitive sport, in room 407 we usually do follow-the-leader games where I create a pattern or structure, and the students try to copy it. If teaching Romy to focus her eyes on the right place during regular PE was challenging, it was practically a non-issue when we did stack cups. Stack cups follow-the-leader may not seem like playing catch or ball-handling exercises, but there are important behaviors common to both:

- Hand–eye coordination
- Partner or group cooperation
- Turn-taking
- Patience

I wait until my students are sitting at the table facing me. I have several 3-stacks in different patterns and colors. One at a time, I ask students to choose a stack by color or by pointing, and I hand it to them. Then I begin to model patterns, and they copy them.

- Stacked right-side-up
- Stacked up-side-down
- Unstacked in a row
- Arranged in a triangle
- Pyramid
- Spatial relationships: next to, over, under

The next stage may be to hand each student a fourth, fifth, or sixth matching cup. We explore more complex patterns, count cups in rows, request additional cups, take turns, and watch each other. I choose tasks based on my knowledge of my students and on the behaviors that I have pre-taught. I like to stay with a lesson unit for four to six classes. That translates to two or three weeks with two classes per week. When we do a stack cup unit, I meet my students in their classroom where we typically spend ten minutes before returning to the gym. Once in the gym, we do our locomotor activities, but I also try to do something that allows us to practice what we were doing earlier. That includes using the same language. Instead of stack cups, we might be distributing balls or hula hoops, and my students must request a color. Then we play follow-the-leader. I model, and they copy me. Over time, the language and cues we practiced in the classroom transfer to the gym.

The difference in students' behavior when they are in their classroom and when they are in my gym is sometimes striking. Students who tend to stim and wander in the gym are calm and purposeful in the classroom. They appear comfortable around their own desks, chairs, cubbies, and materials. This is not to say that they aren't comfortable and excited to be in the gym. However, the transition to a space they haven't seen for 3–5 days, the openness and the sensory differences can make it difficult for a student like Romy to focus. Interacting with Romy in her own classroom gave me an important perspective. It allowed me to see what was possible when she was calm and comfortable. Room 407 has such a calm and orderly atmosphere. It is well organized physically, and smooth cooperation and coordination among the special ed. team is evident. Students exhibit a lot of independence and work focus. The ambience feels calm in contrast to the way things often feel in PE. The fact that every student is usually occupied with their own task is clearly a reason why. Even though there is more movement, physical energy, and noise, it is possible to create that kind of calm in the gym by compressing the space, creative use of equipment and furniture, adjusting lighting, good teamwork, and routine.

Lesson Plans: Body Awareness and Balance

A note on the SHAPE national K-12 standards and the APENS adapted physical education standards – The SHAPE standards are "designed to be a tool for (physical educators) to use in planning curricula; designing units, lessons and practice tasks; and assessing and tracking student progress across grades." The APENS, on the other hand, are professional standards. They define the content that adapted physical educators should know and practice.

LESSON PLAN: NOSE TO THE FLOOR

Goals: Students move with control in a confined space, maintain different body shapes on different bases of support, be able to identify various parts of their body.
SHAPE Standards:
Standard 1. Demonstrates competency in a variety of motor skills and movement patterns>Non-locomotor Stability (S1.E7[3])

Standard 2. Movement concepts, principles & knowledge>Movement in self-space (S2.E1)
APENS (Adapted Physical Education National Standards):
Standard 1. Human Development>Plan physical education programs that maximize opportunities for integrated group play (1.03.06.02)
Standard 2. Motor Behavior>Select and design activities to help remediate deficiencies in proprioception[4] (2.01.04.05)
Standard 10. Teaching>Understand the effectiveness of using the command style of teaching with individuals with disabilities (10.01.01.01)
Setting: An inclusive gen. ed. activity.
Background: Suitable for primary grades but can be adapted for older students. Related to musical chairs. Ideal for primary grades and English Language Learners to practice names for parts of the body.
Equipment: A circle large enough for all students to move around in comfortably without colliding. Enough flat bases or poly spots for every student. Music.
Description: Students must always remain inside the circle. While music plays, students walk about or perform a motor pattern as instructed. When music stops, teacher calls out a body part. Students must find a base and place that part of their body on it.
Challenge Option: Call out difficult body part combinations like foot and shoulder. Reduce the number of bases. Increase size of play area and spread bases farther apart.
Inclusivity and Modifications: Since this is a group activity, there is no pressure on any individual. If unsure what to do, students can copy their classmates.

LESSON PLAN: BALANCE STATIONS

Goals: Students practice various balances, students work independently by following picture card models, students work with a partner and exemplify appropriate helping and coaching behavior.

SHAPE Standards:

Standard 1.Demonstrate competency in a variety of motor skills and movement patterns>Balance, Weight Transfer (S1.E7,8)

Standard 4. Personal responsibility>Working with others (S4.E4)

APENS:

Standard 10. Teaching>Understand the effectiveness of using the reciprocal[5] style of teaching with individuals with disabilities (10.01.02.01)

Standard 10. Teaching>Design activities and instructions to the ability level of the individual such as using picture activity cards to depict the desired skill to be performed (10.01.03.01)

Standard 10. Teaching>Design the class activities in a circuit type or station arrangement (10.01.03.02)

Setting: An inclusive gen. ed. activity.

Background: A versatile station rotation. A good standalone or lead-in activity to a tumbling or gymnastics unit.

Equipment: 5 × 10′ gym mats. Large station cards or posters available from various suppliers or create your own. Create partners or groups of three making sure that each mat can accommodate one group. A countdown timer.

Setup: Arrange mats end to end in one or more long rows depending on number of stations and size of room. Place an activity card illustrating a balance next to each mat.

Safety: Review your tumbling and floor work rules around personal space, maximum number of students per mat, and falling hazards.

Description: Explain and demo balances as necessary. Students perform different balances at each station as directed by station cards: on one foot, hand and foot, 3-points, V-sit, on stomach, airplane on one leg, knee and hand, double knee, plank, side plank. They stay at a station until the signal to rotate.

Inclusivity and Modifications: Most students prefer to work with partners when given the choice. A para can be a partner. There is no competition as students challenge themselves to perform each balance.

Challenge Option: Partner balances with students supporting each other.

Functional and Socializing Skills, Outdoor Play Structures

From talking to Romy's teacher and reading her IEP, I knew that an important educational goal was to help her socialize with her peers. In the context of PE that meant an ability to be around others in play situations and to develop the kinds of skills that would enable her to participate in simple activities. Recess is a favorite time of day for all elementary children. It was also the time when Romy's para support person could take a step back and give her more space to enjoy her unstructured and (relatively) unsupervised time like everyone else. It was the only time when she was free to interact with students in other classes and they with her. Many students' IEPs contain goals around socializing with peers. Independence from adults, showing interest in others, initiating conversation, maintaining appropriate personal space, respectful interaction, and turn-taking often apply to play situations. In an elementary school, recess and playground are where much of that behavior takes place.

We had good adult coverage with the Firefly class. They came to PE with at least two and sometimes three paras, depending on the class makeup on a given day. If we went outside for PE during recess, there would be challenges due to the crowding, but there were also benefits and opportunities to interact with peers. The paras and I could deploy to different locations to support any students who needed to learn the interaction and recreation behaviors that are important on playgrounds. Camille and I discussed how PE time could be used for this. We decided that the playground slide would involve many of the skills. If students learned the sequence of climbing a ladder, standing on a platform, waiting their turn, going down a slide, running back, getting in line with other children, and sliding again, many of our PE and functional goals would be met. Our outdoor play structure had both steps and ladders leading to the upper level, which contained a variety of features. There was a wiggly rope bridge, a "firehouse" pole, a cargo net, a steering wheel, a megaphone, and two slides. Our students enjoyed various of these options, but a few were not comfortable on the slide.

We had several incentives for students who made progress: school store tokens, lunch with the principal, preferred activity, extra recess time. The process of overcoming the initial fear of going down the slide was different for each student. Using incremental steps tended to be effective. First sit on your bottom then scoot to top of slide, dangle feet over the edge, high-5 an adult standing to the side, go down slowly behind a trusted adult or friend, allow student to choose a buddy from our crew of Playworks student monitors.[6]

Elizabeth was an outgoing, friendly, and gentle fourth grader. At recess, she enjoyed imagination games and play acting with her friends. She climbed the steps to the platform but was not comfortable on the wobbly bridge and was fearful of the slide due to balance issues caused by a vision disability. She was careful and deliberate when going from a standing position to a seated one and vice versa. Our first step was to examine the slide from all angles. We took turns sitting on the bottom end. We turned and knelt on it and crawled up as far as she was comfortable. We ran our hands up and down it. We walked back and forth under it. We gave high-5s to students as they slid past us. We climbed up to the platform and approached the slide and stood against the railing watching other students as they took their turn, and we commented on their different styles. We did this for two PE periods without any intention of going down the slide, but we talked about how much fun it looked. Being familiar with Elizabeth's balance issues, I wanted her to try a seated position when she approached the slide. On the third day, Elizabeth stood in line with other students, and when it was her turn, she sat down on her bottom and scooted to the edge, taking time to experience the view, but she wasn't ready to go. I helped her scoot back. After watching several more students one of her buddies approached the slide and encouraged her. The buddy went first but held her position part way down the slide, and Elizabeth followed.

A note on technique. Working with students in the gym and on the play structure often involved having to influence and persuade students to move. By this time, I had learned some techniques for getting students with autism to move, change position, and change direction. You can accomplish a lot simply by using your posture and proximity without touching a student. When a student loses interest in an activity, they often walk away. Grabbing them is clearly not an option and telling them to stop and come back is often ineffective. So, what I do is stay with the student and steer them to the desired location by interposing my body and preventing them from going in any other direction. I don't consider it to be "corralling." I think of it as communicating the direction that I want us to go in a language he or she understands, and that we go there together, side-by-side. Maybe this is a subtle distinction, and you are not overly concerned with how it looks but just that it works. I would respond that *I need to know the justification for the techniques I use with students when I'm outside the boundaries that I'm accustomed to with my neurotypical students.* If I don't know the justification for close proximity or physical guidance, I feel I'm at greater risk of transgressing a student's rights and/or diminishing their dignity, not to mention running afoul of the rules that govern my employment.

Think about It Questions

Think about ways you share who you are with students. List some of the skills, experiences, interests, and cultural traits that you have shared. Try to include less-tangible traits such as your communication style and the ways you approach relationships. Can you cite examples of how students have benefited?

How do you decide how long to do an activity like a drill or skill practice? What are the factors that go into your decision? If your answer depends on the class or specific students, explain.

Whether you teach in a gym or a classroom or are itinerant, think of an activity or lesson that might benefit from moving to a different location than where you usually conduct it.

You are teaching a class with very diverse learners. You have an idea for a new activity. How do you decide whether it qualifies to be part of your curriculum, or not.

What are your warmup routines? How do you modify them for students with special needs? What features do you or could you add to make them more challenging or interesting?

When you have a student who is accompanied by a support professional, are your expectations clear to both the adult and the student in the following situations? Be as specific as possible by describing the paraprofessional's purpose, location and expected behavior.

- ♦ You are talking to your class.
- ♦ You are demonstrating a skill such as the proper way to use a resistance band, and students are copying.
- ♦ Your students are doing a pair activity like tossing and catching.
- ♦ Your students are performing a station rotation in small groups.

Notes

1 Bosu is the trade name for a type of half-spherical balance platform. They are about three feet in diameter, have a hard plastic bottom and a heavy-duty inflatable dome. They are adaptable to all kinds of

calisthenics, isometrics, and balances. You can place them dome-side-up or -down for more challenge. The name stands for "both sides up."

2   It is a good idea to have several types of rewards to offer when your students earn them. While Mario's favorite equipment was razor scooters and 4-wheeled scooters, Patrick's preferred activity was pushing a rolling cart around the gym. Esther was eclectic and athletic. She loved jump ropes and balls – the bigger the better – and she also loved any kind of tumbling activity. The key is to know what types of activities you can use for positive reinforcement rewards with all your students. Block (2016, p. 319) has a Reinforcement Survey for finding out exactly what appeals to your students.

3   S stands for "standard." E stands for "elementary" level.

4   Sensory information arising from within the body, resulting in the sense of position and movement, similar to kinesthesis.

5   Working with a partner and receiving feedback from partner based on criteria prepared by the teacher (NCPEID 2020).

6   Our school received grant money to hire a company called Playworks. Their staff trained a cadre of fifth graders to be recess leaders. These students learned how to give their peers positive support, setup and supervise games, lend a helping hand, and be a friend to students who needed one. The whole school felt more upbeat when recess conflicts and confusion were reduced by providing this student leadership and structure.

6

Fitness Activities for Better Health

PE teachers recognize that their students exhibit a wide range of abilities as well as a wide range in their levels of health and fitness. We take this diversity into account when we plan activities and games. However, it becomes apparent that students with disabilities are sometimes so far to the bottom of this range that it is challenging to adapt activities for them. How does one overcome these challenges when it comes to supporting health and fitness? I pursue the same strategy that I always use when I have knowledge gaps about my students.

- Look for goals and targets in the IEP.
- Talk to those who know my students' fitness and health status best (on the staff these would be the classroom teacher, the nurse, the physical therapist, and occupational therapist).
- Establish rapport.
- Observe closely.
- Refer to my fitness curriculum (Materials sometimes offer ideas for working with students with disabilities, including alternative assessments.)
- Find tasks that are measurable.
- Employ trial-and-error modification.

Fitness Components

If I could boil down all the things we teach and practice in PE about fitness into a few basic principles, the **Five Health Components of Fitness** would be at the top of the list. These five health-related components of fitness are the centerpiece of our PE curriculum.[1]

- ♦ Flexibility
- ♦ Body composition
- ♦ Cardiorespiratory endurance
- ♦ Muscle strength
- ♦ Muscle endurance

One can think of them as the health concepts underlying all the lessons in the PE teacher's playbook, and they are broad enough to be relevant and adaptable for students with diverse abilities.

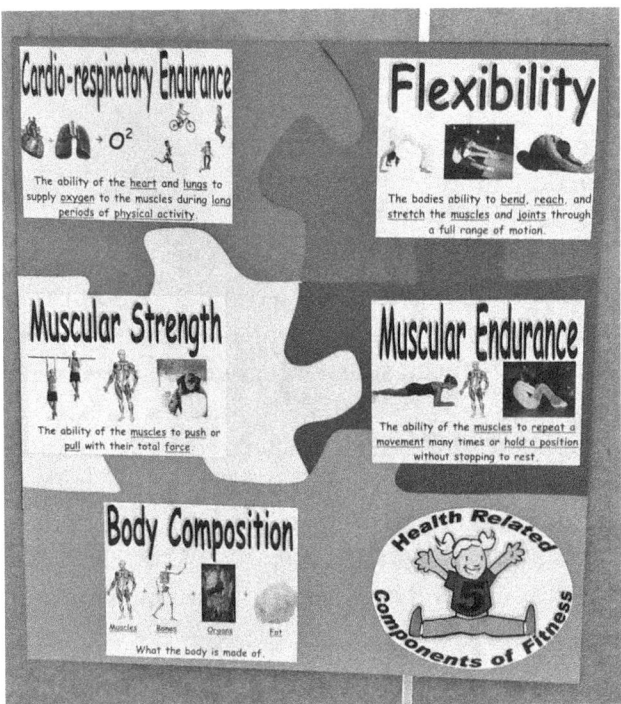

FIGURE 6.1 Five Health Components of Fitness.

We evaluate performance with respect to these components, we set goals, and we emphasize the importance of self-assessment and self-knowledge so that students can make informed choices about improving their personal physical fitness. All of us face challenges to personal fitness: available leisure time, lack of guidance or models, access to appropriate space and equipment, ingrained habits, upbringing, health and injury, physical and mental individuality. Exposure to a wide variety of enjoyable physical activities is a big part of the solution to staying fit when there are so many obstacles.

Our elementary PE team recognizes the **Six-Skill-Related Fitness Components** as an adjunct to the five health-related fitness components because they further define the locomotor and non-locomotor skills that we want our students to develop. Pangrazi (2004) initially identified five areas and added a sixth (reaction time) in 2007:

- Balance
- Agility
- Speed
- Power
- Coordination
- Reaction Time

He noted that differentiating between the health components and the skill components makes it easier to develop appropriate fitness goals and objectives for youngsters who he assumed would not need many advanced skills or higher intensity exercise:

> Health-related fitness is characterized by moderate and regular physical activity...Skill-related fitness is the right choice for people who want to perform at a high level, but is less acceptable for the majority of people because it requires training and exercising at high intensities.
> (p. 231)

Our elementary students do not restrict themselves to low-intensity levels of exercise, and they do acquire some very advanced motor and sport skills. Major content areas for upper elementary and middle school, grades 4–7, include locomotor patterns used in sports, dance, and leisure activities as well as advanced manipulative patterns such as volleying, dribbling, and punting.[2] The Five for Life curriculum we use for upper elementary students specifies three essential training variables for fitness: frequency (sessions per week), intensity (training load expressed as resistance, speed, or heart rate), and time (minutes or repetitions). **Intensity** is broken down into five different levels, from low to maximum, which correspond to heart rate ranges expressed as a percentage of maximum heart rate:

> Intensity Level 1 – Media/Seat, Heart Rate below 40% of maximum
> Intensity Level 2 – Daily Activity, Heart Rate 40–50% of maximum
> Intensity Level 3 – Base, Heart Rate 51–65% of maximum
> Intensity Level 4 – Heart Health, Heart Rate 66–85% of maximum
> Intensity Level 5 – Max, Heart Rate above 85% of maximum

A big part of the academic content in PE is understanding intensity levels and heart rate so that students know how to monitor their own activity for improved fitness and health. Our students routinely take heart rate measurements after warmups and cardio exercise. Even kindergarten students have a basic understanding of their heart function and know that their heart beats faster when they work harder. I ask them to count their heart "thumps" after a run while I time them, and they love to call out their numbers, accurate or not. Many of our fourth graders and most of our fifth graders learn how to measure their heart rate by counting their radial (wrist) or carotid (neck) pulse for a 10- or 15-second interval, and then referring to a wall chart that does the multiplication conversion to a true heart rate (beats per minute). When students crowd around the wall charts, fingers track across the numbers, they share information out loud, they compare, and they show pride in their ability to do this on their own. Students whose understanding of these principles is still developing, listen, observe, and glean information. I observe this part of the lesson closely, listen to students' comments, and keep a lookout for those who need extra help. Years ago, I invested in heart rate monitors; when the batteries failed, however, I stopped using them in favor of the low-tech method above because the monitors did all the thinking for students and eliminated the collaborative aspect of the exercise as well as the valuable life skill of taking one's pulse. Our Heart Health Stations (we have three spaced around the gym so an entire class can get access to the information quickly after exercising) include clear visuals and definitions of essential vocabulary: heart rate, resting heart rate, maximum heart rate, and percentages of max heart rate by age. The last chart shows students the correlation between heart rate and workout intensity and identifies the "healthy heart zone" range. The discussions that ensue are very valuable. There are so many take-aways and potential questions, and there are ways to conduct these discussions so that students can keep their information private. Instead of saying, "Raise your hand if you reached the healthy heart zone after the warmup," I might say, "Wiggle the big toe on your right foot if you reached the healthy heart zone."

After fifteen minutes of soccer drills or scrimmages, we want our students to be able to identify which health-related fitness components they were practicing. We remind students that a particular lesson or practice will usually contribute to more than one component, and the discussions we have as we identify those components are important learning opportunities. The *balance* and *agility* required for an activity like soccer leads us naturally into a discussion of skill components that are important in games and sports. Having realized how essential those skills are to ball control, we plan workouts we think will help such as agility ladders, obstacle courses and dance.

Flexibility and Locomotor Activities

Flexibility activities are a favorite with many students. Not surprisingly, the students who display exceptional flexibility are usually those who do dance or gymnastics. Many of them can sit on the floor with legs outstretched and lay their head on their knees. Their performance on the Sit and Reach test is *way* above standard. The test equipment consists of a table with inches marked on top, and as the student reaches forward, he/she pushes a slider that travels up the scale. Most gen. ed. students meet standard on this test. However, many of our students with disabilities score below standard. For some, it is because they don't attain the correct form for the test which involves locking the knees. Others can get into the correct position but do not lean into the stretch. Non-locomotor flexibility exercises are difficult for many students. Therefore, we try to incorporate a flexibility component into other activities.

If a task has an intrinsic incentive, students pursue it with more enthusiasm. We have a magnetic measuring board on the gym wall that can be used to measure stretching as well as jumping ability. While standing flat-footed or on tiptoes, students reach up to place a magnet as high on the metal meter board as they can. Several factors make it attractive to students: the magnets, which come in an endless variety of shapes and colors, the tactile experience, the sound of the magnet on the metal board, the immediate visual feedback of seeing the height they reached in feet and inches. For many students, the competitive aspect is also appealing.

A flexibility stretch station rotation is an obvious way to learn and practice a variety of stretches and can be configured as a partner or small-group activity. Our curriculum materials include a box of 11 × 17 laminated cards that illustrate locomotor and non-locomotor tasks in the five fitness areas, including flexibility, and I post a different one at each station. Most PE teachers in our school district include yoga in their curriculum, usually as part of a unit on flexibility. I enjoy being on a mat among my students and prefer modeling the poses myself to projecting computer images, but I have done both. There are many online applications that model appropriate yoga poses for children. In my personal practice I find that assessment and measurement have a limited role, but I can assess students in ways that still allow them to practice in the proper spirit: with calm and patience. Knowing that yoga improves flexibility and muscle strength, I choose poses and balances for different parts of the body:

- Head turns and chin tucks for the neck
- Sitting cross-legged and butterfly for quadriceps
- Toe-touch or downward dog for hamstrings
- Cat-cow and sphinx for the back
- Clock face stretches for shoulders (face or stand sideways to a wall and stretch out arm to the different clock positions)
- Mountain, stork, and tiptoe balances work the entire body.

Assessment is straightforward. I assign a simple rubric designating important elements: "no evidence, some evidence, mastery" to indicate a student's ability to attain a pose for a given time. The climbing wall is a flexibility workout in disguise. When students are on the wall, their incentive is to get higher and farther. Stretching is simply like walking or jumping. It is just a way to get where you want to go. It does not bother me that flexibility on the wall cannot be measured as precisely as with the Sit and Reach equipment. Distance traversed or height reached are totally legitimate assessments.

Challenge courses provide another opportunity for working on flexibility. There are several factors that make them much more interesting to students than static stretching:

- Soft surfaces
- Colors
- Multiple shapes, textures, and heights
- Varied travelling modes: walking, leaping, sliding, rolling
- Interaction with classmates

To assess the flexibility component of a challenge course, I identify a portion of the course and a discrete task such as bending over a shape or rolling like a ball. Jumping stations are also good assessment points. Students who can jump from heights generally have good flexibility since a comfortable landing requires

FIGURE 6.2 A student stretches over a half donut on the challenge course.

them to flex and roll. Clearly, one's ability to jump from a height and land safely is determined by other factors in addition to flexibility, but it contributes to the overall picture.

Lesson Plans: Body Composition and Nutrition

Unlike the other four fitness components, body composition is not something that we practice directly, but we do talk about its importance. I tell students that when we take care of the other fitness components and pay attention to nutrition, body composition takes care of itself. The definition of body composition provided by our PE curriculum is "The ratio between fat mass and fat-free mass in the body." A fitness plan that includes cardiorespiratory endurance and resistance training will improve body composition. Cardiorespiratory endurance activities are recommended because when the body increases its demand for oxygen, it burns calories at a much faster rate. Resistance training is recommended because it builds fat-free mass. The more fat-free mass the body has, the faster it will burn calories.[3]

Identifying the food groups is one of the foundational goals in our nutrition unit. I often kick off the topic with a nutrition version of a typical jogging warmup.

LESSON PLAN: FOOD GROUP LAPS

Goals: Students gain knowledge about the food groups and expand their awareness of food choices. Students gain practice in tossing and catching while performing a locomotor movement.

SHAPE K-12 Standards:

Standard 1. Demonstrate competency in a variety of motor skills and movement>Locomotor>Jogging, Running (S1.E2)

Standard 1. Demonstrate competency in a variety of motor skills and movement>Manipulative>Throws underhand, Catches (S1.E13,16)

Standard 3. Demonstrates the knowledge and skills to achieve and maintain a health-enhancing level of physical activity and fitness>Nutrition (S3.E6)

APENS:

Standard 1. Human Development>Utilize cues and prompts that are appropriate to the instructional and/or behavior needs of the individual with a disability.1.05.03.02

Standard 1. Human Development>Plan physical education programs that maximize opportunities for integrated group play (1.03.06.02)

Standard 10. Teaching>Implement instructional and environmental cues based on the needs of individuals from least to most intrusive. (10.02.01.01)

Standard 10. Teaching>Identify a variety of age-appropriate social reinforcers that may appeal to individuals such as smile, high five, shaking hands. (10.06.05.01)
Setting: An inclusive gen. ed. activity.
Background: Prior discussion of food groups is recommended.
Equipment: A poster that displays a variety of foods organized by group is a helpful reference. About 5 light gator balls of one color that symbolizes a particular food group such as green for vegetables, blue for dairy, orange for grains, red for fruit, purple for protein, yellow for fats and oils, black for empty calories like candy.
Setup: Tell the class which food group will be involved and explain that the balls are a color that represents that food group. Explain that 4 or 5 students will stand in the center of the track, each one with a ball, while the rest of the class jogs around the outside. Their job is to toss a ball to a student who calls out a food that is a member of the designated food category and then trade places with that student. To receive a toss, a student must call out an appropriate food and must be jogging. As they pass each other they must show spirit by offering a high five.
Description: On the teacher's signal, the class starts jogging and calling out foods. The tossers toss the balls and switch places with the catchers. Monitoring and modeling by the teacher are best accomplished by participating in the activity rather than watching from the sideline.
Inclusivity and Modifications: Since this is a group activity, there is no pressure on any individual. Students hear their classmates call out examples of foods and watch each other if unsure what to do. We call it "research," not copying. Frustration arises when students do not

get a ball tossed to them either because they are not calling out a food, or they are calling out a food that is not in the right category. You can remedy this by posting the food group poster close to the track or by carrying a stack of food cards and handing them to certain students with the proviso that they can only use it once and then must pass it to another student. It's also the case that once inside the circle, students often favor friends. Every teacher has methods for addressing this. Any method that involves establishing a rule ahead of time is preferable to repeatedly reminding students to share with everyone.

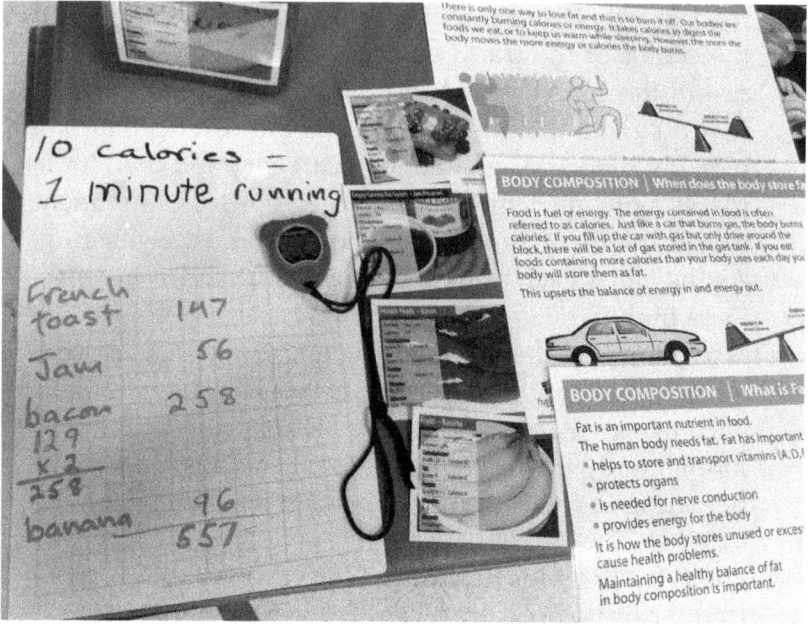

FIGURE 6.3 Academic Content: Nutrition and Body Composition.

We also do a cardio workout that accurately simulates the seesaw relationship between calorie accumulation and exercise:

LESSON PLAN: CALORIE BURNER

Goals: Students gain knowledge about food groups and calories. Students reinforce their understanding of the variables affecting body composition – calories consumed/calories burned. Students gain practice in tossing and catching while performing a locomotor movement.

SHAPE K-12 Standards:

Standard 1. Demonstrate competency in a variety of motor skills and movement patterns>Locomotor>Jogging, Running (S1.E2)

Standard 2. >Non-locomotor>Weight Transfer>mule kicks, mountain climbers, burpees (S1.E8)

Standard 3. Demonstrate the knowledge and skills to achieve and maintain a health-enhancing level of physical activity and fitness>Nutrition (S3.E6)

APENS:

Standard 1. Human Development>Plan physical education programs that maximize opportunities for integrated group play (1.03.06.02)

Standard 2. Motor Behavior>Modify activities to accommodate for differing patterns of performance for fundamental motor skills exhibited by some individuals with disabilities. (2.01.10.01)

Setting: An inclusive gen. ed. activity.

Background: Once students can identify the groups that common foods belong to and have a basic understanding of calories or fatty foods, body weight, and exercise, then you are ready to play. I do this with students as early as first grade.

Equipment: A set of food cards. A large food group poster is optional but is helpful as a reference during the workout.

Setup: Discuss foods that are high in calories and that when you take in more calories than you burn through exercise they are stored as fat. Choose a non-locomotor exercise like burpees or mountain climbers as the designated "calorie burner." Designate a different number of repetitions to each food group. For example, 1 rep for vegetables, 2 reps for fruit, 3 reps for protein, 4 reps for grain, 5 reps for dairy, 6 reps for fats and empty calories. Here is where a food group poster with the reps indicated on sticky notes can serve as a helpful reference.

Description: On a signal, students begin jogging. When I blow the whistle, I hold up a food card and call it out. Students stop running, identify the food group and the appropriate number of exercise reps, do the reps, and then continue jogging.

Inclusivity and Modifications: Since this is a group activity, there is no pressure on any individual. Students may call out the answers and watch their classmates if unsure what to do. I also offer alternative locomotor options to jogging by placing different cardio stations inside the track such as step boxes or jump rope, and we have a specially designed trampoline with handlebars for students who have difficulty walking.

Choosemyplate.gov is an excellent resource for visual aids. A set of Choose My Plate food mats coupled with a stack of food nutrition cards are very handy for learning nutrition-related academic content. Food cards that are illustrated with full color photos are best. They should designate the food group, and list all the important nutrition facts (recommended daily allowance, calories, and nutrient content) just as you would find them on any food label. One of my students' favorite activities is the **Choose My Plate Relay**. Each group of two or three students has a Choose My Plate mat and is allowed to "shop" for a set number of food items at the supermarket (usually a circle in the center of the gym where the food cards are spread

FIGURE 6.4 Choose My Plate Tea Party.

out). Their assignment is to create a breakfast, lunch, dinner, or snack by arranging food cards on their plates. The discussion that takes place among the teammates as they argue their food preferences and categories is the most valuable part of the activity. Meanwhile I visit each group, thank them for inviting me to their house for a meal, and we talk about the food they have prepared. They love this kind of domestic pretend game, and who doesn't like to talk about food?! We also do a variation in the form of a Tea Party[4] in which the teams rotate around the gym and stop at each plate for a minute to comment on the choices that other teams have made. Colorful laminated Choose My Plate mats, posters and realia are available from many suppliers.

Cardiorespiratory Endurance, Running, and Other Options

Why is there so much running in physical education? Partly because sports and playground games usually involve running but also because there is no more important foundation to health and fitness than cardiorespiratory endurance, and running is an easy and equipment-free way of getting there. Some students do not like to run, but there are ways to use incentives that help performance. Making activities fun is incentive enough for most students, but it often requires some research to discover the incentives that work for my students who have autism, are neurodiverse, or sensory diverse. For some, a favorite toy, fidget, or the company of a preferred adult can be the reward for completing work. I had a student who did not like our jogging warmups, but he liked to hug and hold hands. However, he had to learn that only certain times were appropriate. I led him around the track at a pace that pushed his endurance, staying just ahead of him, and when he caught up to me, he was allowed to hold my hand. We can also use equipment as a motivator. Poly spots, step boxes, beams, and hurdles are a few of the pieces of equipment I've added to the track that make a big difference in students' enthusiasm and intensity level.

Classroom teachers are always happy to share methods they use to motivate students and adopting these gives them consistency between class and PE. Students learn to become independent when they use tracking tools to monitor work completion. These can be as simple as a calendar or assignment list with check-off boxes. *The Autism Fitness Handbook* by David Geslak describes effective use of countdown boards for monitoring repetitions during exercise. Some students may prefer a more tactile, 3-dimensional tool utilizing marbles with trays or boxes.

Sports and chasing/fleeing games have a built-in cardio element. However, PE teachers today know that a significant portion of our students are either averse to or lacking the ability to engage in competitive and sometimes aggressive as well as potentially humiliating activities. We don't eliminate these, but we can adapt them and find additional options to make them more inclusive. *Physical Education for Students with Autism Spectrum Disorders* (2014) includes a version of tag in which high-interest equipment plays an essential role. Tag sticks with soft foam hand shapes and inflatable wands supply "the extra visual cue to help students with ASD understand the 'it' in tag games." With these props, accidental pushing will also be less likely. I had a young man in PE for several years who had ASD. He loved tag games, but he perceived intent on the part of his classmates that was not always accurate, and he was very sensitive about being tagged or targeted. I tried giving him "protective armor" in the form of a colored vest which identified him as a non-target. However, he eventually saw that being tagged and doing the calisthenics was part of the fun. The best approach was to chat before the game to see what modifications he and I could agree on and then continue to check in with him during the game in case we needed to make changes.

LESSON PLAN: STOMP TAG

Setting: Enjoy a chase and flee game that is less aggressive than a typical tag game.

SHAPE K-12 Standards:

Standard 1. Demonstrate competency in a variety of motor skills and movement patterns>Locomotor>Travels showing differentiation between sprinting and running. (S1.E2.3)

Standard 2. Applies knowledge of concepts, principles, strategies, and tactics related to movement and performance>Recognizes the concept of open spaces in a movement context. (S2.E1.3)

Standard 4. Exhibits responsible personal and social behavior that respects self and others>Exhibits personal responsibility in teacher-directed activities. (S4.E1.3)

APENS:

Standard 1. Human Development>Plan physical education programs that maximize opportunities for integrated group play. (1.03.06.02)

Standard 2. Motor Behavior>Understand common deviations in the development of the tactile system among individuals with disabilities>Develop and implement programs to enhance individuals' abilities to tolerate various levels of tactile stimuli. (2.01.04.03)

Standard 2. Motor Behavior>Understand how appropriate modifications of the physical environment enable individuals with disabilities to perform sport skills. (2.01.12.01)

Standard 10. Teaching>Create activity opportunities with variable levels of success to enable all individuals to achieve some measure of success in the same activity. (10.01.04.01)

Background: This is a favorite game at every grade level, and it is also inherently inclusive. Players do not tag each other. Instead, they target a piece of tape or ribbon that is tucked into their shoe so that the target is an object and not the person. By avoiding aggressive physical contact, conflicts and accidental collisions are rare.

Safety: Review and demonstrate your safety rules for tag games (personal space awareness, permitted modes and speed of travel, in-bounds and out-of-bounds lines, appropriate use of equipment for tagging, no targeting or ganging up on specific students.)

Equipment: A 3–4-foot length of caution tape for each student, boundary cones

Description: Chase and flee while trying to "tag" classmates by stepping on their tape so that it pulls out of their shoe. Consequence for losing your tape is a specified number of non-locomotor exercises, after which students can replace their tape and continue the game.

Inclusivity and Modifications: (Explain modifications to the class prior to play.) By increasing the length of a student's tape, thereby increasing the size of their target, the teacher can challenge skilled players. By reducing the size of the tape or even eliminating it completely, the teacher can ensure that a student will not be targeted. **A key inclusion principle is to design activities that do not make a student stand out or feel different.** Therefore, the teacher may include a rule requiring that all players who have not been tagged after five minutes must use a longer tape. You can apply this creatively by giving certain students a piece of tape that is a tiny bit longer than what they had. Modify the calisthenics students do when they are tagged. Change the level of difficulty and/or number of repetitions to accommodate students.

One of our jobs as PE teachers is to make sure our students understand how cardiorespiratory endurance benefits health and fitness and that almost any physical activity that raises heart and breathing rates can lead to improved cardiorespiratory endurance (CRE). Knowing a wide variety of activities that accomplish this is helpful not only because "variety is the spice of life," but also because each one (jogging, line sprints, jump rope, swimming, biking, stair climbing, etc.) involves different skills and muscles. So, in PE we practice as wide a variety as possible so that students are more likely to discover a CRE activity that they enjoy and excel at for years to come.

These also happen to be among the most challenging activities for many of our students. Many students stop running before they raise their heart rate significantly, and they often lack the strength and balance for repeated jumping. An option is to use a fun piece of equipment like a trampoline or balance ball. We know that repetitive exercising of large muscle groups throttles up respiration, heart rate and improves endurance. For example, we can disguise a cardio workout in the form of non-locomotor balance ball play:

- Balance on your stomach like Superman
- Balance on your back and raise one arm, one leg, an arm and a leg
- Do crunches
- Invent balance poses

FIGURE 6.5 Using Equipment Adaptations to Access the Climbing Wall and Make It More Inviting.

As long as students stay balanced on their ball, they are working large muscle groups. While there are cardio work-arounds for students who do not run for long duration, running is so much a part of life that we want students to try to improve at it and enjoy it. This is where your experience and ingenuity are important.

The solution to getting Romy running pretty much presented itself. Romy's father was into soccer and had been practicing with her for several years. One day we were out on the grass field passing a soccer ball back and forth, and we started walking side-by-side, continuing to pass the ball. I started to walk a little faster, and Romy kept up. Gradually I broke into a jog, and with her focus still on the soccer ball she jogged along with me. We sustained the passing game for over a minute until she was breathing harder. That was the first time I had seen Romy perform an aerobic workout. With each student the path to working up to an aerobic workout is a little different. It's a question of gradually pushing a little faster, a little longer, a little farther until you find a sustainable pace without pushing so hard that your student loses interest. Eventually, Romy and I were able to pass a soccer ball for five minutes, which I considered a very adequate cardio component of her PE lesson. If I had had Romy for another year, one of my goals would have been to step away and have other people, particularly students, partner with her.

Muscle Strengthening Activities and Physical Prompts

It would be nice if there were a single exercise, sport or piece of equipment that provided a workout in all five fitness areas and that was age appropriate for my students. But there is not. That is why cross-training is such a popular way to stay fit. In PE we design lessons around the fitness components depending on what we want to emphasize on a given day. I have found that with young students the hardest component to address is muscle strength. Older students can safely learn to use free weights, multifunctional equipment, and universal machines – all those cool-looking items that are off-limits to children. However, there are options: tumbling, bear and crab walk, balance balls, climbing walls, bars and play structures. These exercises enable students to get a muscle workout by leveraging their own body weight. Importantly, they also involve locomotion, which is almost a prerequisite for keeping energetic young people engaged. Climbing walls are excellent muscle strengtheners, but for some children, including first-time learners, timid students, and some with disabilities, you must do more than just say, "Climb!" The appropriate learning prompt for some students will involve physical assistance. You may have to place their foot on a protrusion or even support their weight until they engage with both arms and legs. This is the justification for what, to skeptics, might seem like intrusive physical contact used with students.

Some students do not support their weight on the climbing wall or lack the strength and body control for balance balls and tumbling. I decided to dig deeper into the possibilities of using resistance tubes. With resistance tubes, I felt we could explore a wide variety of muscle challenges. I soon learned that, as with most PE and fitness skills, learning how to use a resistance tube would be an incremental process. It would also stretch my imaginative use of learning prompts to the limit. I introduced this new activity on the learning circle.

To start, we spent about five minutes a day handling the tubes and letting students experiment with them. They liked to swing it like a propeller, and we obviously had to limit this behavior. Gradually we explored the tube's stretching properties. Several students wanted to pull and let go quickly, but the adults deployed in such a way that we could control it. We would hold the opposite end and pull, always trying to sense the limit where a student would let it snap. We did not want them to experience that sensation, or worse, start to enjoy it. We reinforced students' grips with our own hands, when necessary. It didn't bother me that we were relieving them of some of the pulling effort. It mattered more that they experienced the proper way to use the equipment. Gradually we loosened our hold and let students take more of the strain. Advancing to the point where a student could sustain a pulling force was our first goal.

We did overhead triceps extensions and chest presses with the tube behind our backs and under our arm pits. However, when students had to anchor the tube with feet or knees, progress was slower. For bicep curls, we anchored our tubes by standing on them. I modelled how to keep my weight bearing on it. We assisted some students with subtle pressure on their back to help keep them over their center of gravity and prevent the tube from slipping out. In this situation, with safety the priority, a teacher might maintain the pressure on the student's back and shoulders. They might even face the student and place their own foot on the tube. We tried gradually reducing assistance until students were working 100% independently, anchoring securely and doing curl-ups. "Fading" is the term used for removing scaffolds, supports, or prompts that a student no longer needs. A support that is faded signifies a skill that is learned.

Next, we attempted a shoulder press by anchoring the tube on the floor with both knees, but it often slipped, and I decided to look for a different method of doing presses that would be safer and would also work for pull-downs and rowboats. With resistance tubes or bands there are two main safety risks. The first is letting the band snap and hit yourself or someone else. The second is uncontrolled release of tension so that your limb is ballistically yanked back, which can cause injury to joints. A safe and secure anchoring method that I learned from going to physical therapy is to loop the tube around a doorknob, draw the two handles to the other side of the door and shut it – making sure it's latched. If the doorknob or handle is at the wrong height for you, an option is tying a knot at the tube's midpoint and closing the door past the knot. I liked this setup because students would not need to anchor their tubes, and if they let go of the handles, they would hit the door and not one of us. Other benefits of anchoring this way were that it would leave our hands free and allow us to do presses safely by facing away from the door. What I discovered when we tried this was that we couldn't just start up with presses where we left off with biceps curls. The motions are opposite and involve opposing muscle groups. So, we went through the same steps that we did at the beginning: experimenting with the tube, testing the new position, then transitioning to controlled pulling. For some reason, pushing did not come as naturally as pulling did. Perhaps it was because it meant facing away from the door where the tube was anchored. With some students, facing them and applying opposing force resulted in a pushing contest, which is what I had hoped, but not always. These are the kinds of puzzles that interest me, not just as a teacher, but in general. It's like when you're working on some project in your garage or trying to do a home repair, and you don't have the part you want, but you know that if you put your mind to it, you can figure out a workaround. It turned out that an understanding of muscle anatomy was the key.

My gen. ed. classes spend significant time on basic anatomy. We have college-level posters from Carolina Biological that convey a realistic view of the muscular and skeletal systems. Our curriculum has an academic component that describes the various muscle locations and functions very nicely. We have a set of laminated cards that show students not only how to perform over 100 different stretches, cardio and muscle exercises but also includes diagrams that show the specific muscles that are activated with each exercise. The written text, the visuals and our discussion are mutually reinforcing. However, I found that when I first learned that I could actually feel my own biceps contract when I did a bicep curl, was when I really *believed* that muscles worked the way the texts said they did. That is why I have all my students probe and squeeze their own biceps, triceps, and quadriceps as they pull, push and squat so they can feel the muscles harden and bulge. This was going through my mind when I couldn't get students to push the resistance tube handle away from their body. So, I tried helping a student push with one hand while squeezing the back of their upper arm, thinking that perhaps their triceps would "wake up" and connect to the pushing motion. I can't be sure, but this may have helped one or two students to do chest presses and shoulder presses. We would do six or eight repetitions while adults counted and gave lots of praise. When a student pushed, I could feel their triceps contract, and I gave immediate positive feedback.

Some people reading this may feel that what I'm describing is an "inappropriate" level of physical contact with students. When you work with students who have special needs you will confront this question, and you should decide what kinds of contact you can justify based on a student's IEP, learning needs, and parent permission. The key word here is "decide." It's better to follow a conscious decision-making process when performing actions that are not customary or that cause you to question their appropriateness. That process should include consultation with colleagues. Earlier I mentioned that paraeducators have more "meat and potatoes" contact with the room 407 students than anyone in the school. Most people could not imagine the true extent of the contact that is required (and authorized) to support some students. It will come as a shock to many teachers that today in public schools paraeducators, special education teachers, and even the occasional principal are diapering students on a daily basis. I have talked to these wonderful, committed educators about it and asked what they thought about this being part of their duty. Incredibly, I always get the same response – a shoulder shrug and an answer like, "It's just another part of the job. I'm used to it."

Preserving our students' dignity and modesty is something that special educators take very seriously. Think how private and easily shamed your son or daughter might have been about their body at the age of ten or eleven. Would it be right for someone not to be afforded the same dignity just because their disability prevented them from regulating their behavior according to social "norms?" With some students, this was very challenging. Their stimming behavior could be quite inappropriate. When it occurred during PE, I tried to use the same vocabulary and phrases that adults practiced in room 407 to call the student's attention to the behavior and correct it such as, "Hands down. Not here. That's for home." As always, we cannot rely solely on verbal communication. Special educators employ quite a few hand signals to reinforce their words. When students put their hands in their mouths, paras gesture with two fingers on each hand pointing to their own mouth and repeatedly lowering fingers to their waist. If it was not appropriate for me to engage a student with a particular correction, I called a para's attention to the situation. We tried to shape the behavior and control it. It was difficult to eliminate it completely.

To reiterate, when you find yourself having physical contact with a student who has special needs or with *any* student, you need to know that you have valid justification. To do it just because you've always done it, and it's never been a problem before, is not an educationally sound reason. If environmental, verbal, or gesture prompts prove ineffective, physical guidance that helps a student avoid failure or confusion can be justified (Block 2016, p. 112). When Gillian, our school principal, authorized occasional one-on-one PE classes with certain students, she was very clear in her justification: The student's needs were not being met in gen. ed. PE or in our smaller, specially designed PE class. Gillian believed that even though it was neither customary nor advisable to have teachers alone with students, there had just been a technology upgrade in our building that she felt would protect us in the event of a "He said; she said," situation: That was the installation of security cameras in all the common spaces, including the gym. I take a lot of pride in the things we accomplished in our fitness units, and I am very gratified for the trust that developed between me and the students while we pushed the boundaries. In many ways, I discovered how to do PE along with my students.

Think about It Questions

The resistance tube unit involved a lot of physical contact. Was there a point where you said to yourself, "No way that's appropriate. I wouldn't do it." Explain.

Is there anything that you do with your students for which you've ever doubted that there is any actual justification? Have you ever considered whether something that you do with your students might not have a contractual or legal basis? Find someone (*trustworthy!*) who you can discuss this with.

Think of one of your students who has challenges in PE related to the Five Health Related Fitness Components or comparable health/fitness principles from your curriculum.

- Rank the fitness components from easiest to hardest for your student.
- List examples of your student performing activities related to each component.
- Come up with new activities for each component that you might introduce your student to.

Your principal has observed one of your units and noted the amount of physical contact between you and students. They asked you to email a weekly note to parents describing your activities and explaining the justification for using physical learning prompts such as those used during the resistance tube unit. Draft a note and share with a colleague or parent.

Notes

1. Cowan et al. (2013).
2. Wessel and Kelly (1986), as cited in Block (2016), p. 14.
3. Cowan et al. (2013).
4. A Tea Party, like a mingle, is a versatile instruction technique simulating a social gathering in which students are required to interact and acquire information from each other.

7

From Non-Locomotor to Locomotor

Transition from the Learning Circle to the Track

The Firefly class is are on the black learning circle. My three "dependables," Grant, Nanda, and Mario, are on their poly spots, another student is wandering, and two students are in the vicinity of their spots with paras working to get them into posture. Kayden is one of those two. I have choices. I can wait until the other two are on their spots. I can buy time and talk about the medicine balls. I can ask students questions to get their focus while we wait. I can start instruction with the three students who are in posture, or I can leave the circle and try to bring our wanderer back. Kayden is calm and halfheartedly holding his ball. His para keeps trying to push it into his hands, but he keeps relaxing his grip. I flash on an image of Velcro gloves and ball – an idea to file away for another time. Kayden is nearly in posture, and that decides it. Without speaking, I raise the ball over my head then bring it down to my chest and repeat. Grant and Mario are copying me nicely. Nanda is chatting about going down the mini slide in the corner. "Eyes on teacher!" one of the paras reminds her. I start counting reps, and all three paras immediately join the chorus. Mario and Grant count too. Kayden is smiling and doing a little dance. His medicine ball is an annoying distraction that

DOI: 10.4324/9781003437901-8

the para won't take away. John Handy's "Hard Work" is playing over the PA system. A third para has finished her break, enters the gym, spots Esther in the far corner about to climb a stack of gym mats, and jogs down there. We've done several reps overhead, then side to side, then around the waist and behind the back and finally figure eights through the legs. That took about four minutes. I call out, "Follow me," and head away from the circle with the ball above my head. They are close behind me, and we return to the track to continue Follow the Leader. We repeat the same maneuvers that we practiced on the circle, but now we're also walking, side-sliding and even jogging. With the addition of the medicine balls, the laps are less tedious (notice I didn't say easier!), and the combination of weights and locomotion makes this a good strength and endurance builder.

The first minute of an exercise is always the best. It's new, no one is tired yet, no one has lost interest yet. So much of our effort – mine and the paras' – is just supporting and cheerleading. We use encouraging language and try to keep in mind the axiom that positive reinforcement is not just "happy talk." It lets the student know exactly what it is they're doing right. We use their names, we exaggeratedly model the movements, we push, we prod, we hold on, we dance. We do everything we can think of to entice our students into and through the activity. We are also trying to enliven the atmosphere, which serves an instructional purpose. Happy, energized people tend to be better workers and better learners.

Can we just be adults for a minute? As the one in charge, I have a responsibility to my support professionals. I want PE to be fun for them too. I want them to enjoy their time in the gym as much as possible, and their enthusiasm will transfer to the kids. So, when the students are constructively engaged, we joke around and share adult humor just to keep it light. I know how tough the rest of their day is. After all, we are all adults. I don't change who I am just because I happen to be teaching six-year-olds. I never use a baby voice or a mommy/daddy voice, I never refer to myself in the third person. Sorry, but I need to go on a bit of a rant here. Why on earth do some primary teachers refer to themselves in the third person?!?! You're in school, not at home.

These are not your babies. Model accuracy. Model directness. Avoid confusion. If your young students are very immature, expect more – not less – of them. Even if your first graders have no English language learners among them, their brains are still constructing grammar and syntax. Think about the *reason* you resort to the third person when you are teaching. Is it because you are feeling self-important? impatient? confused? exasperated? If that's the case, then deal with the cause.

I adjust my vocabulary, simplify my grammar and concepts, but I use the same voice with first graders that I do with everyone else. Because I was an ESL teacher for fifteen years, I can't help paying a lot of attention to communication and language. If I were to put my "ESL hat" on for a moment, my number one piece of advice to teachers would be **1. Talk less. 2. Talk less.** I don't want to be "buddies" with my students. When I look back on my best teachers and professors, they were definitely *not* my "buddies."

The Mat Circle: Locomotor

The **"mat circle"** is an ideal location to transition from non-locomotor to locomotor movement. It serves the same gathering and instructional function as the learning circle but enables us to practice different kinds of activities. The prep is simple: a hexagon made up of folded gym mats. I usually place them so that they are touching, or nearly so. This gives us comfortable seating for up to twelve people facing each other. Even when folded, the mats are wide enough to stand and move around on comfortably without fear of losing one's balance. With a class of six, plus three paras and myself, everyone gets plenty of assistance.

When we go to the mat circle after our laps, I like to start with everyone seated. The non-locomotor version involves seated work with balls, action songs, and conversation. The locomotor version is more active. We usually begin with a step routine. I step down to the inside and then up and backwards and repeat about a dozen times as we count together. I use short, descriptive phrases to keep it clear and simple. "Down, back up.

FIGURE 7.1 Train Time. Teacher Leads Students around the Mat Circle.

Down, back up…" With an arm around her waist, one of the paras assists Gemma up and down. Gemma waves her ribbon, and her eyes wander about, but she does step up and down, for now. Next, we modify so that we step backwards from the mats down to the outside then back up. The whole time we face into the circle so that we never lose eye contact.

After steps, we usually do some type of yoga-like balances and poses – standing tall, tip toes, tree, stork, airplane. Then we make believe we're a train on a track and follow each other around the mat circle. If there is a gap between mats, some students step down and up, but others, like Esther, love to jump the gap. We practice stopping, starting and about-face. I have a tub with playground balls or soccer balls stationed close by. We stop the train, and I roll a ball to each student when they are in posture (seated and looking at me). I may ask them what color ball they want. Some days we use medicine balls for the extra muscle workout. They imitate me as I hold the ball over my head, swing it to the left and to the right, make rainbows, hold

FIGURE 7.2 Students roll medicine balls inside the mat circle.

it between my knees and count to "5 alligator," hold it between my feet a few inches above the floor and count again. The mats define our space and provide structure for a variety of exercises and games. Instruction is followed by practice and independent play. Students roll balls back and forth inside the mat circle. The contained space keeps the balls in play and holds their focus well.

It's important to remember that an activity doesn't have to be an "all-or-nothing" proposition. If students wander away from the mat circle, we don't necessarily have to abandon the concept of a learning circle. If the mat circle is not a strong enough learning prompt to maintain students' attention, I can change the space more dramatically. As I mentioned earlier, returning to room 407 to do small motor activities could be very effective for students like Romy who tended not to visually focus on the task that was front and center. That would be an option for Gemma's class, but what if I wanted to do some gross motor work? There is no rule that says you may not bring chairs into the gym. Once they are seated in their familiar learning posture, I can give each student a medicine ball or dumbbell. When Esther starts to get up out of her chair, a para reminds her, "Feet on the floor. Eyes on teacher." Sitting in chairs, we can do many of the non-locomotor activities that we would do at the mat circle: arm lifts, leg lifts, stretches, with or without weights. We can get a complete abdominal workout. Being seated in a chair, or at a desk, is a powerful environmental prompt. There is no reason not to use it in settings outside the classroom if it works.

Stepping with Modifications

For a cardiorespiratory workout I often opt for step boxes. Each student has their own step box on the Learning Circle, and even though I stand on top of mine, the students may take a different position initially. Several sit, some may jump up and down and others may even flip theirs upside down. Patrick sometimes got on hands and knees and started to push his along the floor. One way to avoid off-task behavior is to launch right into steps along with a song or chant. I find that automatically engages most students, whereas if I stand, wait, and ask for appropriate behavior, I am less likely to get the result I want. A music soundtrack with a good beat helps with motivation. Any type of follow the leader game provides a good workout. Replacing the step boxes with Bosu balls is a good follow-up. The wobble makes them more of a balance challenge so that virtually all muscles in the body are firing just to keep from falling off.

After a few minutes of solo exercise, I like to create a partnering opportunity, so I remove half the step boxes with the music still playing, which cues us to keep moving. We encourage the students without equipment to partner up. This is a difficult transition for some, like Patrick, who are very disappointed when I remove their equipment. The challenge is for partners to keep stepping up and down while sharing a smaller space on the box, and this creates more balance and cooperation opportunities. Now, my job is to observe and to see where we have enough success to start changing step patterns and fading support from some of the paras who may be holding onto students and coaching. A student like Patrick, who has not only balance and mobility challenges but also an intellectual disability, needs a lot of adult support to participate. I tried different approaches to find one that works and meets my goals for him. His balance was good when walking, but static standing and sitting positions were challenging. He had difficulty holding and gripping objects. Complex movements like tossing and catching were not yet emergent. Locomotion in different modalities, games, calisthenics, fitness equipment, travelling on uneven surfaces, and independent exercise all required significant adult support.

What would your expectations be for the step box activity with a student like Patrick? If the amount of physical support to assist them onto a step box is excessive, modify:

- Put a chair next to their step box for them to hold onto.
- Replace the step box with something flatter like a mat or a scooter.
- Have them sit rather than stand.

Being in the learning space and in proximity to classmates without necessarily performing the same task can fulfill IEP goals for some students. This was often the case with Patrick.

Sometimes using familiar equipment in creative new ways is a solution to a problem. Agility was an issue with many of the Fireflies. I continually tried to add new steps to the warmup. After forwards, backwards travel was next, and, after that, side slides, but slides tended to be much harder to learn. The problem was that aside from my words and modeling, there were no environmental cues to help them grasp the correct body position and rhythm for side sliding. Beginners tend to cross their legs or turn away from a lateral orientation because the movement is unnatural. I explored ways of narrowing the travel path so that there was only enough room to move sideways. My students are

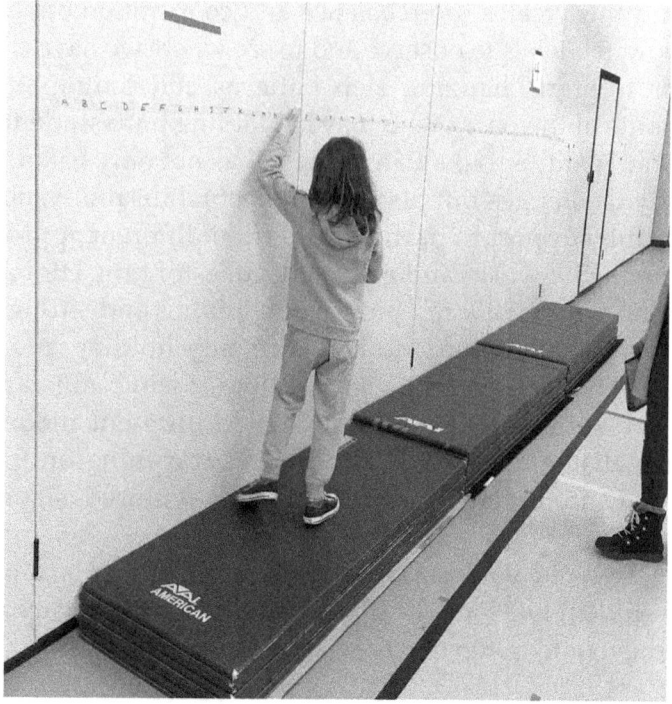

FIGURE 7.3 Using environmental prompts to encourage a student to sidestep.

very comfortable walking on folded mats. While I would have preferred something narrower, their three-foot width and ten-inch height creates a fun travel platform. Mats by themselves would not be enough of an environmental prompt to travel sideways, so I tried to think of things that would encourage students to orient their bodies, and particularly their arms and hands, to move laterally. I placed four folded mats end-to-end against a wall and stuck a long piece of yellow tape to the wall at eye level. I wanted something with more texture that they could run their hands along, but that was the best I could think of. I added visual cues by writing the alphabet, then numbers and then geometric shapes on the tape.

I planned to teach side slides after mat circle time, so I placed the two stations close to each other. The mat circle is familiar to my students and expected behavior is pretty much mastered.

They are also in a seated position with three adults sitting among them which makes it easy to communicate and reach out a helping hand or discourage off-task behavior. When it was time to transition, I held up the Velcro schedule poster that showed a new card after mats: "NEW!" I told them to watch me and demonstrated how I walked to the left end of the blue mats, stepped up with my right foot, put both hands on the yellow tape, and walked sideways while reciting the alphabet letters. The second time, I asked Angelo if he wanted to go next, and he jumped up immediately and followed me, hands on tape, reciting letters. He did cross his feet, but I did not expect perfection the first time. Of five students present that day, only one did not do the new task. I was very happy with four out of five.

Wheels

After crawling and walking, riding is the next step in the passage to independence. Moving faster with less effort: a dream realized by means of wheels. When I started teaching PE, the square four-wheeled scooter was the vehicle of choice among the elementary school programs. Within a couple of years, the early adopters began to acquire larger round models. The wheels were bigger and had quality bearings, the colors were brighter, a fifth grader could fit their whole body on one comfortably, they attained greater speeds, and they were self-stacking with wheels nesting in the deck handles of the scooter underneath. (Thank you from all PE teachers for this feature!) Within months, the rest of us knew we were using obsolete technology, and we started purchasing the round models as fast as we could afford to at the price of about $65 a piece. When I roll a five-foot stack of these scooters out of my office, students go nuts. It immediately turns exercise into fun. When we do scooter relays, they propel themselves as fast as they can using arms, legs, and abdominal muscles. If given a choice between a team game like kickball or scooters, it is ironically only the top athletes who tend to choose the ball game. They gravitate toward more competitive situations because of their self-confidence. Everyone else chooses scooters, including most notably, the students whose PE skills are below grade level.

Most of my students viewed scooters as a treat, but some lack the flexing and extending coordination in their legs or the upper body strength that allow them to propel themselves on a scooter by pushing against the floor with feet while seated or walking while leaning forward onto the scooter. Patrick was among those students who, with adult assistance, could sit on a scooter and extend his legs with intent to move but needed help. Chandra attached a length of rope to his scooter and towed him across the gym. That solved one problem: He was moving and experiencing the sensation of riding on wheels. However, he was not getting much of a muscle workout other than the effort it took to stay seated on the deck. I thought we could do better. My goal was for my students to learn to move under their own power, but I had to find a way to adapt the equipment for them.

I had been using a kind of homemade self-powered rope tow in my PE classes for several years. I have two pull-up bars that I use as anchor points on the wall and tie a 25-foot length of thick, soft rope to each one. The students sit on an upside-down carpet square which slides well on our floor, grab the end of the rope, and pull themselves to the wall. They naturally turn it into a drag race. It is bizarre, competitive, and hard work, and they love it. I decided to adapt it for students with diverse abilities. A scooter substituted for the carpet square and would offer a fraction of the resistance. All my students grasped the rope, but even with Grant, Mario, and Nanda as examples to follow, some either dropped it or did not pull on it. It could be that they were not ready for the concept of pulling on an object to move their body. I thought we could try another technique – a modification that would reduce the amount of dexterity required to handle the rope. The idea was to fix the rope at both ends and suspend it like a tight rope two to three feet above the floor. Putting tension on it made all the difference. Students pulled themselves along it, ducked underneath it, pulled on it like a bowstring – all while moving on scooters.

FIGURE 7.4 A suspended rope provides assistance on scooters.

Ball Striking

Sometime in the late winter or early spring I like to start my classes on a ball-striking unit. By this time, we've done lots of throwing and catching exercises plus games like basketball, wallball, and flickerball. Now it's time to explore the wide variety of striking activities. There are sports that involve striking a ball with a body part, like volleyball, soccer, and handball, and racket sports like ping pong, tennis, racquetball, and badminton, but there are also dozens of fun games that present fewer barriers to inclusion, like popcorn, straddleball and punchball. Based on their experience with gen. ed. classes, a PE teacher wanting to introduce students to kickball might set up one or more bases, have students stand behind home plate in a line, and roll the ball to them. However, for some students that may be an advanced expectation. Whether the sport is striking with hands as in volleyball or feet as in kickball or soccer, a more reliable first step is to focus on the most important skill and ignore, for the present, all other requirements and rules. Breaking tasks down into their components when students are learning them is almost never a bad idea. Therefore, giving each student a ball and modelling the enjoyment of kicking it around the gym with freedom and enthusiasm is a logical first stage to a kickball unit.

If stoppages were a challenge when we played catch, they would be an even greater problem in hand/paddle-striking activities. Students would have to surmount the difficulties of hand–eye coordination to contact the ball, and we couldn't realistically expect much accuracy toward a target. Clearly, we'd spend more time chasing balls than hitting them. For our first striking lesson I gave each student a light Styrofoam paddle and a tub of wiffleballs and let them hit away. Various images like crazy faces taped to the wall helped them to focus on the target. When their tubs were empty, students had to retrieve their balls and start over. This was fine as an introduction to striking. Some students had success hitting balls out of their hands. Others tried tossing and hitting, but their tosses weren't accurate. Nanda lost patience with the paddle, picked up the balls, and threw them. Esther picked up her tub and dumped all the balls. Some students were more interested in emptying the tub as fast as possible rather than striking. Knowing my students, I had pretty much predicted how this would go, but it was at least a start, and I had a sense of the kind of changes I would have to make for them to be more successful.

As a fisherman, a wiffleball tied to a line on a pole was the first idea that came to mind. The ball would never escape, and students would not have to hold or toss the ball with one hand and hit it with the other. It would be a more natural swing. Since a ball on a string would be in constant motion, they would really have to concentrate on it. The haphazard approach they took with the balls in the tub would not work. Using actual fishing rods would be impractical. I know that I wasn't willing to donate any of my gear to the cause. However, any kind of wooden pole would probably work. If we had three or four setups, the paras and I could hold them while the students swung, but that meant

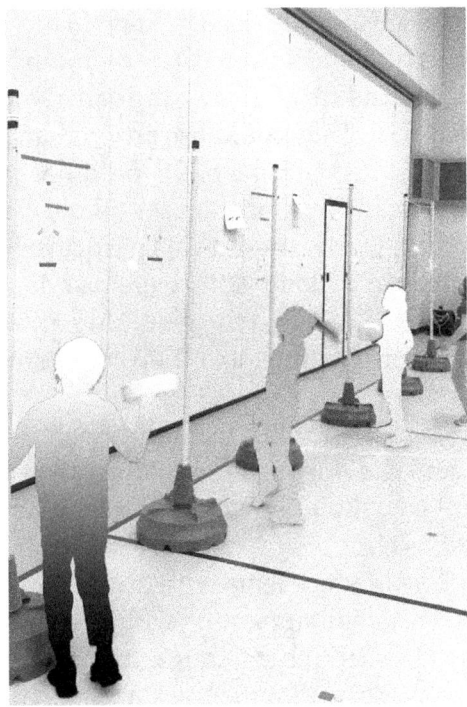

FIGURE 7.5 Paddle Tetherball. Wiffle balls are tied to a string that is looped around a rope which is suspended between volleyball standards.

we would not be able to assist them with their posture and swing. Somehow, we would have to mount the equipment on the wall or on a fixed structure. Sometimes an idea comes to me if I just stare long enough at all the equipment and paraphernalia we have in the PE office.

I remember the day my multi-tethered-ball apparatus was set up in the gym, and my 8:30 gen. ed. class saw it for the first time. They couldn't wait to get at it. I had prepped a station rotation of different paddle activities, one of which was the tether apparatus. It had been easy to put together. I set up all our volleyball standards in a straight line about six feet apart and connected them with a clothesline twisted a couple of times around the top of each pole. I tied the first standard to a hook on the wall so that one end was securely anchored. I tethered wiffleballs in the spans between the poles with three-foot lengths of one-eighth-inch nylon cord. To prevent the cords from twisting the clothesline, I used loops instead of knots. The volleyball standards could be raised and lowered to accommodate the height of my students. I found that hanging the ball a few inches above eye level worked well. They could use an overhand swing which comes naturally to kids, and the ball would not hit them in the face. It was terrific hand–eye practice for all my classes – kindergarten through fifth grade – and it was particularly appealing to those students whose striking skills were just developing. They never had to chase the ball, and the pendulum motion seemed to make the target more inviting, *and* they could smack it as hard they wanted.

The Fireflies came to PE that afternoon with no break between them and the previous class. That is not an ideal situation. If possible, you should have at least five minutes to break down the previous class's setup and get ready for any class that is specially designed for students with disabilities, or vice versa. I knew that the tetherball apparatus would distract them when they came in, so I pushed the standards and all the station equipment against the walls, set up the track and the mat circle while the paras led them in their warmup laps. After the laps and mat activities, I pulled out the tether ball standards and gave each student a paddle. As luck would have it, that day there were four paddle stations and four students. Mario, Grant, and Esther started swinging at the balls right away. Gemma was galloping around the gym. I had never seen Gemma play catch or shoot at a basket or dribble a soccer ball, and I was curious to see if the suspended wiffleball would capture her attention. While I was helping another student correct his grip on the paddle, Gemma walked over and watched us. Even that was unusual. I gave her a paddle and pointed her to a vacant spot. She tapped the ball very lightly as if to test it. She continued to tap it tentatively and watch it swing gently…four, five, six times and more. The paras and I looked at each other with wide eyes, recognizing that this was a first. A couple of phones came out of pockets and began taking videos. These would serve an important purpose by documenting Gemma's behavior for her teacher, physical therapist, and her parents. Once they had confidence in their ability to contact the ball, all my other students wanted to hit it as hard as they could but not Gemma. Her enjoyment appeared to come from watching the ball's pendulum motion and not from smacking it, but I would take this success as a starting point and add complexity with more props, equipment substitutions, and partners. When after much trial and error, a student discovers something they are good at, a teacher will use that as a blueprint for new learning.

Bowling

Earlier, I discussed the inclusive nature of offering multiple targets of varying size and distance so that students can find their own challenge level. I have used this approach in both special needs and gen. ed. PE classes, and it is perfectly adaptable for both. Point values based on difficulty encourage students to challenge themselves. I use multiple targets with rolling, tossing, putting with hockey sticks, and a variety of balls and objects. For tossing, I like beanbags. They are easy to grasp, they have a nice heft, and they don't roll away. I use the term "bowling" loosely. We got a set of regulation bowling pins from a local bowling alley that was throwing them out. Plastic light-weight pins are very inexpensive. I like the ones that have sand in the bottom, since they are more stable. Unless I want to do a specific bowling unit with balls, pins and score keeping, bowling often just means rolling to a target, and there are unlimited modifications based on the needs of my students.

- ♦ Vary the type of target.
- ♦ Vary the type of ball.
- ♦ Vary the size of the target.
- ♦ Vary the distance to the target.
- ♦ Creatively modify the path to the target with carpet, ramps, blocks of wood, hurdles, etc.
- ♦ Vary partner and group configuration.

A consistent feature of almost all our target activities is rotating through several roles or jobs. Students almost never perform all aspects of the task sequence by themselves. Whether we are rolling, bowling, tossing, or golfing I designate roles for 1. The thrower/bowler, 2. The retriever/safety monitor, 3. On-deck. Depending on the size of the teams, we may have double or even triple on deck. Like all PE teachers, I never want to see my students standing around with nothing to do other than waiting. So, if there are multiple on-deck teammates, each on-deck person has a task to perform plus a piece of equipment such as a jump rope, hula hoop, or resistance tube. The retriever/safety monitor's job is to stand behind the target and give the "all clear" sign (two thumbs up) to the bowler when it's safe. When the turn is completed, the retriever/monitor rolls the ball back and resets the target. The on-deck person rotates to bowler, the bowler rotates to retriever/monitor, and the retriever/monitor rotates to on-deck. Consistency of these roles across different activities reinforces the behavior.

Bowling was one of Patrick's favorite games. It contained elements that he enjoyed: multiple pieces of equipment that moved, rolled, and crashed and classmates running and cheering when they hit a target. When it was his turn to bowl, an adult walked with him to the target as he carried the ball and dropped it on the pin, or sometimes kicked the pin over. The initial bowling goals for Patrick were:

- Pick up the ball.
- Walk to the pin.
- Use ball or body to knock over the pin.

Learning to travel from a start location to the target took practice. Because Patrick tended to key on people rather than equipment, it was sometimes effective to use one's location to influence where he travelled. While his para was walking with him toward the pin, he might pay more attention to her than to the pin. But if one partner started him a short distance away while another partner stationed themselves behind the pin and encouraged him in various ways (such as picking up the pin tapping it on the floor and calling his name), Patrick would walk in that direction independently.

Build Learning in Stages: Toss and Catch, Climbing Wall

With his quiet, penetrating stare and visual tracking, Kayden pays very close attention to what is going on in class. He is often in "watching mode" as opposed to "participating mode." For him to transition to active participation, he requires adult support, and Dawn is usually that person. Withdraw the support, and he begins to get agitated. One of my goals was to see what kind of activity he could maintain while Dawn's support was gradually removed. I started with a simple, specific task, established a baseline, and gradually increased the challenge.

Kayden was good at tossing and catching a basketball, so Dawn and I set up a simple three-stage challenge in which she would begin a game of catch with him, then I would sub in for her while she stood by, and finally she would walk away leaving Kayden and me on our own. I stood by as Kayden and Dawn played bounce-pass-catch. Then Dawn handed the ball to me and said, "Kayden, throw to Mr. Mokin." I stepped in and took her place while she stood nearby and watched. I noticed that he turned to look at Dawn frequently as he played with me. After a couple of minutes, Dawn said, "Kayden, stay with Mr. Mokin." She left us alone and went to work with another student. Kayden followed her with his eyes but continued tossing and catching with me, and he continued catching and tossing through all three stages. This was an easily assessable task because it contained a series of binary objectives: accomplished or not.

The next step was to try to expand Kayden's tolerance for group work by including another student and then letting them play on their own while Dawn kept a close watch. It turned out that Kayden was able to do that as well and to enjoy himself if the tasks were repetitive and if we did not ask him to do something unexpected. From watching Camille (Kayden's classroom teacher) and the paras who support him, I have noticed that they did not give him multiple-step directions. Anything we wanted him to do needed to be broken down into separate actions, and we waited until he had completed the first action before giving the second instruction. That meant that we could not tell him to toss the ball to someone if it was sitting on the floor.

The first instruction had to be, "Kayden, pick up the ball." As you have probably inferred, another key to introducing new tasks and skills with Kayden was to teach them in partnership with a trusted adult. Once repeated and mastered, tasks could be combined and performed with other people. There were times when we thought Kayden was attending and engaged and would be open to a new task when he emphatically let us know that he was not. The one element that he always required was the presence of a partner. Learning to work independently would be a goal.

You may think that you have all your activities and transitions carefully planned out, but when human beings are involved, there is always an element of unpredictability. Case in point: The other day, my K-2 Fireflies had completed their warmup on the track, and we were done with our songs and TPR on the mat circle. Our third activity was to be a new climbing wall task. I had already attached short pool noodles in different colors to the wall at different heights and set out colored tubs to match. My students would go to the wall, climb, and retrieve the noodles and sort them into the various tubs by color. I was about to say "All done with mat circle. Follow me to the climbing wall," but stopped myself in mid-sentence. It felt like I was piling on too many expectations. The previous time we had done climbing wall, we did it without the noodle sorting part, and I really wanted to make sure that they understood this new task. In reality, I came to this decision in about three seconds, and just as my students were beginning to stand and head for the wall, I had them all sit down again. I asked one of the paras to take six poly spots from the track and space them out in front of the wall. Here's why: The end goal had multiple elements: climbing, retrieving, and sorting. To convey that understanding I needed students' full attention. To get it I would need them to be still and have eyes on me so I could model all the steps. For the students to be focused, they had to remain in proximity, and based on experience, I knew it would require place markers for them. I directed the students to follow me to the wall and indicated a poly spot for each of them. I saw that only one of six students remained standing on their spot, and the paras were going to have a difficult time containing the learning space, so I had all students sit down, and that helped. When I had their attention, I began modelling the tasks.

Lesson Plans: Upgrade the Track with Variations

LESSON PLAN: DOUBLE TRACK

Goals: Increase challenge level of the track by adding a more complex travel path and locomotor movement patterns.
SHAPE K-12 Standards:
Standard 1. Demonstrate competency in a variety of motor skills and movement patterns>Locomotor>Jogging, Sliding, Skipping, Hopping (S1.E1)
Standard 1. >Manipulative>Catching, Dribbling with hands> (S1.E16,17)
APENS:
Standard 1. Human Development>Plan physical education programs that maximize opportunities for integrated group play (1.03.06.02)
Standard 2. Motor Behavior>Modify activities to accommodate for differing patterns of performance for fundamental motor skills exhibited by some individuals with disabilities. (2.01.10.01)
Setting: An inclusive gen. ed. activity.
Background: DT is a fun alternative to the traditional 4-cone track with some additional features.
Equipment: Eight cones instead of 4. Large exercise cards or posters. Direction arrows.
Setup: Two 4-cone tracks side-by-side. When standing between the tracks think of them as a continuous figure 8 loop. Tracks can be identified by number (1 & 2) or color (red & green). The type of locomotion or travel mode is posted on each track with written directions, diagrams, and/or pictures. For example, track #1: side-slides. Track #2: karaoke step.
Description. Move clockwise on the right track and counterclockwise on the left track so that upon completion of a lap students on both tracks arrive at the middle. At the center point they switch paths to the other track.

Inclusivity and Modifications: Since this is a group activity, there is no pressure on any individual. Students may run with partners or in small groups. More than one locomotor option can be posted so that students can choose. Use a pair of large color cards or posters to help students identify the two tracks.

Challenge Options: Balls for dribbling. Beanbags to balance on head, shoulder, or elbow. Give balls to half the class. Designate only one track for dribbling. When dribblers complete a lap, they pass ball to another student who is finishing the other track.

LESSON PLAN: INSIDE TRACK/OUTSIDE TRACK

Goals: Students perform a complex combination of locomotor and non-locomotor tasks with a partner.

SHAPE K-12 Standards:

Standard 1. Demonstrate competency in a variety of motor skills and movement patterns>Locomotor>Jogging, Sliding, Skipping, Hopping (S1.E1)

Standard 1. Demonstrate competency in a variety of motor skills and movement patterns>Non-locomotor>Balance, Weight Transfer (S1.E8)

Standard 4. Exhibit responsible personal and social behavior that respects self and others>Shares equipment and space with others, Rules & Etiquette (S4.E4,5)

APENS:

Standard 10. Teaching>Understand the effectiveness of using the reciprocal style of teaching with individuals with disabilities (10.01.02.01)

Standard 10. Teaching>Design activities and instructions to the ability level of the individual such as using picture activity cards to depict the desired skill to be performed (10.01.03.01)

Standard 10. Teaching>Identify a variety of age-appropriate social reinforcers that may appeal to individuals such as smile, high five, shaking hands. (10.06.05.01)

Setting: An inclusive gen. ed. activity.

Background: IT/OT combines the cardio locomotor activity of a track with the non-locomotor muscle endurance challenges of calisthenics.

Materials for the Outside Track: 4 cones and large activity cards or posters.

Materials for the Inside Track: 6–8 large station cards with any required equipment (step boxes, jump ropes, resistance tubes, Bosu balls).

Setup: Place 4 cones to create a large rectangular track. Within the outside track, arrange the inside track stations in a circle with station cards facing the center. Number of repetitions is posted on each card. The inside track stations should form a large enough circle so that half the class can exercise inside the circle. Every student has a partner.

Description: While one partner does the inside track, the other partner does the outside track. Predetermine how many laps the outside partner does before switching with the inside partner (usually 1 or 2). They high-5 every time they switch. Examples of outside tasks: jog, side-slide, backwards, lunges, scooters, dribble basketball or soccer ball. Examples of inside tasks: All stations with the same fitness component (cardiorespiratory endurance, flexibility, muscle strength, etc.) or multiple components.

Inclusivity and Modifications: Most students prefer to work with partners when given the choice. A para can be a partner. Permit some partners to stay together and not have to separate to different tracks. Change activity cards to adjust for diverse abilities.

Mat Work and Challenge Courses

My favorite part of any lesson is not the direct instruction. Rather, it is what happens afterwards. If I lay the groundwork properly and provide the right setup, my students are motivated to get busy. I remember something that one of my professors said during a lecture on teaching methods. "As a teacher, you don't want to be working yourself into a lather. You want your students to be working *themselves* into a lather." That image captures the spirit of a classroom happily engaged in the pursuit of learning. With my students absorbed in their work, I am free to observe, provide one-on-one help, and plan the next instructional steps. When I assess my special education classes for time-on-task, the multi-skill/multi-mat challenge course is the most effective kind of lesson. There is not a single student who won't eagerly kick off their shoes, climb, crawl, and roll on mats. In addition to about a dozen tumbling mats, we are fortunate to have three wedge inclines, several attachable foam balance beams, stackable trapezoids, a couple of cylinders and a small plastic slide. We can configure these to make a variety of balance and tumbling stations which can then form the nucleus of an even larger challenge course with the addition of poly spots, step boxes and Bosu balls. The tumbling section provides a muscle strength and balance workout while the poly spot trails and step boxes naturally encourage cardiorespiratory activities like jogging and leaping. The beauty of this kind of equipment is that students are self-reliant on it because it's obvious how each piece of equipment can be used. I can control the type of exercise and get students to engage different muscles and skills simply by switching out equipment. I cut old hula hoops in half and plant the ends into cones to create tunnels for low-to-the-ground travel. I experiment with different layouts: compact, spread out, linear, circular and watch how each setup challenges my students' skills and workout intensity. PE, and teaching in general, is a lot of trial, error, and modification. That is why having an inventor's mindset is central to the job.

With any challenge course, the first step is to preview the activity. When I place signs along the course with graphics, pictures, colors, numbers, and vocabulary words, I have an opportunity to introduce matching and reading tasks. Sometimes I hold duplicates of the cards, show one to a student and ask them to go to that location in the course. I also turn it into a game by mixing the cards up in a tub so that students pick one at a time, and it directs them where to go. Knowing that Patrick was practicing sort and match by color in his classroom, I added color cards to the stations which helped him to be more successful. We walked through the course together while he held a color card so that we could compare it to those on the course and find a match to the station I wanted him to do.

I wish I'd been more aware of the possibilities of tumbling/challenge courses about ten years ago when Tina was in my class. Her mobility challenges were more severe than Patrick's. Tina wore leg braces, and she was able to crawl but could not stand up on her own and used two crutches to walk. Once she was in proximity to our activity, she dropped the crutches so that she had full use of her hands. That meant that she spent a lot of time on the gym floor, mat, or chair while those around her were usually on their feet. While the contrast bothered me a little, being on her belly and side was normal for her. Of course, if we brought our activity down to floor level, it was ideal for her, and we did that as much as we could. However, at that time the floor work I designed was much more limited than the larger, more varied setups that we had later.

Modifying activities and using equipment that is suited to students' diverse abilities is not just the sensible thing to do. It is required by law. The Individuals with Disabilities Education Act (IDEA),[1] section 300.108, stipulates that states must provide physical education for every child with a disability. Not only must they have the opportunity to participate in the regular PE program at a school, but students must be given access to equipment that is adapted for them. The US Department of Education published a very useful guide for physical education, titled *Creating Equal Opportunities for Children and Youth with Disabilities and Extracurricular Athletics* (Office of Special Education Programs,

2011). While it does not provide the kind of detail one would need to develop an adapted PE curriculum, it does an excellent job of laying the foundation for a good program. In it the authors state that to increase opportunities for participation, barriers must be eliminated. One of the common barriers is the safety and security of the play space itself (wood chips don't allow wheelchair access). Appropriate equipment is another.[2]

One of my students with ASD rarely made eye contact or interacted, and his behavior was often characterized by frequent elopement and wandering, but that changed when he went on the challenge course. Luis enjoyed the freedom to go where he wanted and to roll on different mats, but the high interest and compactness of the setup seemed to improve his attention to others. He looked at classmates who were on the same or adjacent piece of equipment and tracked their movements. We had a large donut shape that could be separated into halves and could be

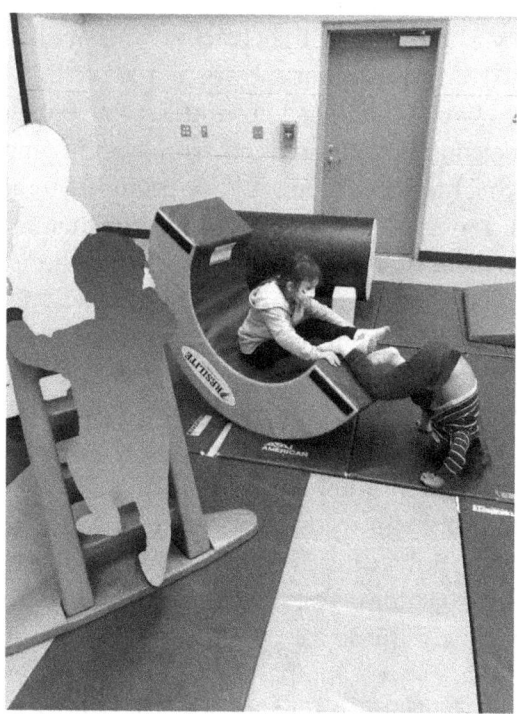

FIGURE 7.6 Students Interacting on the Challenge Course.

stood convexly like a bridge and tunnel or concavely as a rocker. Luis' preferred spot was to crawl inside the donut and wait for his classmates to roll him back and forth. He smiled and never appeared to get dizzy even when they rolled him upside down. Different travel modes (crawling, sliding, rolling, rocking, jumping) are the highlight of challenge courses. Students experience the impact of different surface textures as well as curves and inclines while exerting physical effort. One or more balance beams is almost always a feature in every challenge course. I can adapt for diverse abilities by:

- Modifying the equipment (wider/narrower, lower/higher, shorter/longer)
- Equipment alternatives (balance beam, agility ladder, poly spots)
- Supports and aids (safety bar, chair, partner to help spot)
- Modify the task (1 foot on beam, 1 foot on floor)

I favor PE setups that help students practice cooperation, turn-taking, performance, and audience behavior while working on the five health-related fitness components. Combine that with a design that allows for a maximum amount of independence and minimum amount of frustration and adult interference, and you have an ideal PE lesson. A challenge course is rich in learning opportunities – academic, social, and functional. If I only think of it in traditional "PE terms," my students will miss opportunities. You may not realize the potential connections and extensions that you can include in your lesson until after you've done the lesson once. The next time you use tumbling mats, and a student walks on a mat in his street shoes after you have repeatedly explained the importance of keeping them clean due to the danger of skin infection, you hand them the spray bottle and roll of paper towels. A little to your surprise, they eagerly attack the mat with copious amounts of soapy liquid while the rest of the class watches enviously. Your students have just taught you that they are ready to take on more responsibility.

Tumbling/challenge courses are so effective that I occasionally decide to set one up even when it's not part of my lesson plan for that day. It's a failsafe activity if a lesson is not going the way I want it or if one or more students' behavior escalates, and we need an activity that helps them self-regulate and focus. This is partly due to the way this type of setup radically alters the space and the sensory input. With teamwork, the paras keep students busy while I set up the course. The mats are stacked on 4-wheeled scooters for easy deployment and put-away. In five minutes, I can create a defined and semi-confined space in a corner of the gym with nooks and crannies, soft textures, varied heights, and multiple features that looks like a play fort. The space is a magnet. Elopement is virtually a non-issue. Few intrusive learning prompts are necessary for the Fireflies to use the equipment correctly and to be entirely self-reliant. The equipment itself is an environmental learning prompt. If a student chooses to do a log roll instead of a somersault down the incline, the wedge mat doesn't complain. If they walk with one foot on the balance beam and one foot on the floor, the beam doesn't show disappointment. It's called a challenge course because students challenge themselves and increase the level of difficulty on their own timetable and not according to someone else's expectations. I never see conflicts between students or self-directed anger or disappointment on a challenge course. Students negotiate personal space and turn-taking and discover fun ways to interact on a rolling donut or in a tunnel. They see a classmate do something cool and show appreciation by copying them.

I don't feel that I always need to be "teaching" and controlling. We need to help our students achieve autonomy and self-reliance. Along with having an inventor mindset, this is one of my core values. The world is not made to order for us. It is up to us to create happiness, or at least satisfaction, for ourselves and others.

Think about It Questions

Any situation where someone – a child, a worker, a student – needs to learn a challenging task, a little planning ahead always pays off. In this section you read about a climbing wall lesson that

I broke down into incremental steps to create advantageous conditions for learning. Think of a situation where you had to teach someone something, and the results were not satisfactory. How could you approach the task differently, more methodically?

Choose a scene from the chapter that describe attempts to teach Patrick a skill. Adapt or break down the activity in such a way that you might be able to insert measurable learning. Repeat the exercise with one of your own students in mind.

If discovering that Gemma's interest in tapping a ball on a string is a "blueprint for new learning," what would your next steps be if you were her teacher?

Take a mental inventory of your PE equipment and plan three different challenge courses for a class that has a student in a wheelchair and a student with ASD who is accompanied by a paraeducator.

- A course that requires students to practice various balances
- A course that emphasizes agility
- A course that utilizes partners

Notes

1 The Individuals with Disabilities Education Act. https://sites.ed.gov/idea/
2 U.S. Government, Department of Education, Office of Special Education and Rehabilitative Services (OSERS), Office of Special Education Programs. https://www2.ed.gov/policy/speced/guid/idea/equal-pe.pdf

8

Proactive Strategies for Staying on Task

Playing a Game, and What Happens When It Falls Apart

Our Firefly basketball lesson begins with warmup laps followed by ball-handling practice on the learning circle, then return to the track with balls for bouncing, dribbling, and mini tosses to self. Total time: about fifteen minutes. Now it's time for a game, something that grabs students' attention, creates enthusiasm, involves some fun equipment and challenge. My gen. ed. classes' warmup looks similar: jog and chat for four minutes, heart rate check, grab a basketball from the cart and return to the track. Then they practice multiple variations on dribbling:

- Double whistle = GO
- Single whistle = STOP and FREEZE in the "ready position"
- Triple whistle = switch counterclockwise/clockwise
- Multiple rapid whistles = increase speed

After that we might do a pass and follow drill in groups of five, and then five to ten minutes of shooting practice.

The Fireflies need practice tossing and catching. Every adult pairs up with two students. I tell the paras that we're going to do some rolling, tossing, bouncing, and catching. Dawn is on her own with Kayden, and I'm confident the two of them will be fine. I've seen her play catch with him before, and he enjoys it. He likes basketballs more than smaller balls, and the two of them go right to work. Carol's group has gone into the small vestibule by the gym door. They sit on the floor rolling a basketball back and forth. This spot is perfect: about 10 feet by 7 feet and surrounded by walls and a door on three sides. Grant and Nanda are with me. They are good at playing catch, and therefore they can help provide a model for the rest of the class to follow. I form a triangle about eight feet on a side with poly spots in a corner of the gym. My primary goal is to have a three-way game of catch, but my secondary goals are practicing small-group play and turn-taking. I do not explain what to do. I use minimal, essential input at least until we get going. Paradoxically, I want to see how little "teaching" I can get away with. If I can entice Grant and Nanda to copy me and use their anticipatory set to figure out on their own what to do, then authentic learning is taking place. They are doing the work – not I. Plus, if I start the game with minimal input (to them), I can always add more if they aren't following.

In *The Inner Game of Tennis: The Classic Guide to the Mental Side of Peak Performance*, Timothy Gallwey describes the path he took as a tennis pro to discovering the power of saying less.

"I, too, admit to overteaching as a new pro, but one day when I was in a relaxed mood, I began saying less and noticing more. To my surprise, errors that I saw but didn't mention were correcting themselves without the student ever knowing he had made them. How were the changes happening? Though I found this interesting, it was a little hard on my ego which didn't quite see how it was going to get its due credit for the improvements being made. It was an even greater blow when I realized that sometimes my verbal instructions seemed to *decrease* the probability of the desired correction occurring."

"What happens inside the head between the time the instruction is given and the swing is complete? The first glimmer of an answer to this key question came to me at a moment of rare insight after a lesson with Dorothy. 'Whatever is going on in her head, it's too damn much. She's trying so hard to swing the racquet the way I told her that she can't focus on the ball.' Then and there, I promised myself I would cut down on the quantity of verbal instructions."

Gallwey describes what nonverbal instruction looks like in a tennis lesson. He lets his student know that he is going to skip the usual explanations about grip, stroke, and footwork and instead ask them to carefully watch him hit several strokes and try to grasp a visual image in their mind. Then let their body imitate. The application to gen. ed., inclusion, and specially designed PE is clear.

I bounce pass to Grant. He catches. I look at him and hold up my hands. He bounces the ball back to me. I hold the ball in two hands and look at Nanda. She smiles and raises her hands. I bounce pass to her. She rolls it back to me. No words are spoken so far. Before they start passing to each other, I want to see them practicing the cues: eyes on person with the ball; hands up to request ball. Soon they are passing to me and to each other. Next, I want them to appreciate the fun of random passing. Still, no words are necessary to explain. Here is where I use very exaggerated expressions and gestures. I look at one, then the other. When they raise their hands for the ball, I give them a big smile. I feint a pass to Grant, then pass it to Nanda. They soon catch on. How much complexity should we add? This is the point where I might switch to rolling if the ball starts to escape. It depends entirely on how smooth your progress is and how many stoppages are occurring. One of the biggest hindrances to enjoyable and sustained ball play is the runaway ball. Do your students have the concept of chasing down the ball, returning to the group and continuing where they left off? Only one or two students in the Firefly class do this consistently. Others manage if an adult prompts and accompanies them. The question is: How can you minimize the number of stoppages so that students don't disengage? The simplest strategy is to engineer your play space to prevent the ball from getting away in the first place. That is why I've set up in the corner. I already have two walls. For a third wall, I stand up a folding mat, and that leaves only one open side that I can cover easily. I prefer that to being completely enclosed so I can keep an eye on what's happening in the

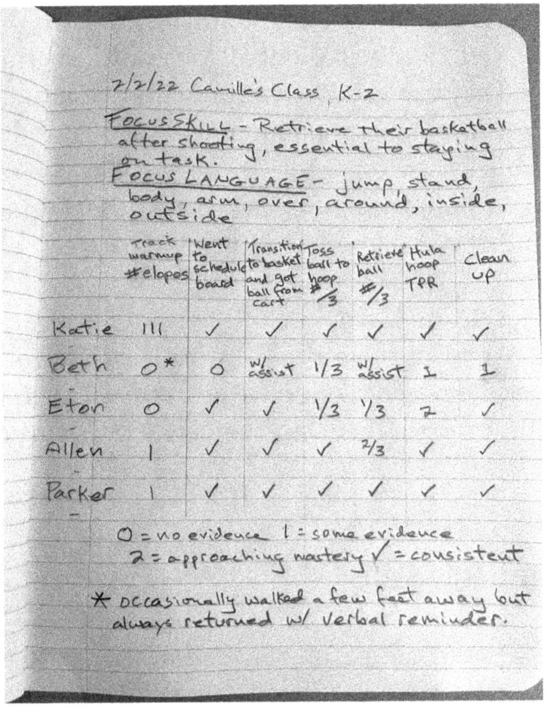

2/2/22 Camille's Class, K-2

FOCUS SKILL - Retrieve their basketball after shooting, essential to staying on task.

FOCUS LANGUAGE - jump, stand, body, arm, over, around, inside, outside

	Track warmup #elopes	Went to schedule board	Transition to basket and got ball from cart	Toss ball to hoop #/3	Retrieve ball #/3	Hula hoop TPR	Clean up
Katie	III	✓	✓	✓	✓	✓	✓
Beth	0*	0	w/ assist	1/3	w/ assist	1	1
Eton	0	✓	✓	1/3	1/3	2	✓
Allen	1	✓	✓	✓	2/3	✓	✓
Parker	1	✓	✓	✓	✓	✓	✓

0 = no evidence 1 = some evidence
2 = approaching mastery ✓ = consistent

* occasionally walked a few feet away but always returned w/ verbal reminder.

FIGURE 8.1 A quick assessment tool for multiple activities utilizes tally marks and checks.

rest of the gym. Now the ball almost never escapes, and we're able to prolong our game for three or four minutes. All goes well until Nanda knocks over the mat and decides that's more fun than playing catch.

The adult in each group can troubleshoot and manage the activity. Chandra knows that Patrick will not sustain interest in ball play and has allowed him to push the ball cart around the gym. Kayden and Dawn are doing well. He smiles and does a little skip-dance every time he passes the ball to her. He is focused on the ball and on Dawn. By comparison, my group looks a little disheveled. Nanda's attention has wandered, and Grant looks sad. I think he gets upset when his classmates don't do what they're expected to. Like many students, he is bothered by the breakdown in "law and order." I tell Nanda that she can help Patrick push the cart and collect the cones and poly spots. She thinks that's a great idea and runs off to join Patrick. Chandra will have to manage the two of them. The group in the vestibule is doing well, so I give the basketball to Grant and bring him over to join them. They can double the fun with two basketballs now. With the amount of time remaining, we'll postpone ball-chasing instruction, but based on what I've seen today, I know that we will have to address those skills if we are going to have success with any kind of ball games. The question I ask myself is,

> Can we teach and learn the skills required to remedy play stoppages and retrieve runaway balls in the context of the games themselves, or do we need to isolate those specific skills, practice them, and set aside the game activity for now?

Prerequisite Game Skills

We elected to incorporate runaway ball practice into our partner tosses and catches, but in a controlled way. Since that is a complex action, I want to make it as simple as possible by designing a partner game that maximizes the give-and-take flow and minimizes the likelihood that balls will escape. There will be less chance of attention wandering away from the game. We'll do that by utilizing corners, walls, or mat barriers and by having partners start close together. We'll also eliminate the chances of bad tosses and catches by rolling instead of tossing to start with. Any time we can teach a new skill by morphing it out of one that is already mastered, we have an advantage. Since students were already very accustomed to the mat circle, that was an obvious place to start the rolling game. We practiced first with the whole class and all adults sitting on the mats and rolling balls back and forth within the circle. Any balls that didn't arrive on target simply rebounded off the mats and remained close enough for someone to reach. Consistent language accompanies the task. It doesn't matter so much what phrase you choose, although simpler is better, but just be consistent. When you first teach a new skill, don't start with "Dorothy, get the ball," and then change to "There's the ball, Dorothy." The next step was spreading the mats farther apart.

We now occasionally had to stand up from our mats to retrieve balls. Finally, we set up mini courts using mats, walls and corners and putting students in smaller groups. Eventually, we hoped to increase the distance between partners and transition to tossing - offering lots of praise whenever students chased a ball.

Engineer the Space

There are different ways to minimize play stoppages. I've utilized all of these, and each has its merits. Elopement was a common behavior that also caused down time, and we were always searching for solutions. It doesn't surprise me that elopement and dysregulated behavior are the most common target behaviors specified in Behavior Intervention Plans. It can have so many different causes, but sometimes your own setup can be partially to blame if it induces students to go where you don't want them to.

We had recently received some exciting new gymnastics equipment and were using it in our challenge courses, and I couldn't have been happier with the results. Students stayed on task longer with less adult interference than with any other activity we had ever done. Paras openly marveled that our students with ASD interacted more on the gymnastics equipment than they did in the classroom. That certainly is a victory when the IEPs of virtually every student in room 407 specify goals around social interaction. The only downside was that it was very difficult for the students to stay in other areas of the gym when they were so attracted to the gymnastics equipment. A typical lesson begins with a warmup around the four cones, then the mat hexagon for sitting and standing calisthenics and songs. With ten to fifteen minutes remaining, we would go to the gymnastics corner. However, we frequently had to prevent students from leaving the track and running to the gymnastics corner. There were several ways to handle this. One para could supervise two or three students in the gymnastics corner while I worked with the other three or four students, or each adult could hold two students by the hand if necessary, or I would be the only adult on the track while one or two paras had the sole job of positioning

FIGURE 8.2 Engineering the Space. A modified warmup track is set up against one wall. paraeducators stand along the open side discourage elopement behavior.

themselves between the track and the gymnastics setup to help contain the class.

After some reflection, I clarified my goals for the lesson and decided that what was most important was for my students to learn that we had a schedule that needed to be followed, and in support of that, we also had a laminated picture poster on the wall that depicted that day's lesson activities in order. Therefore, I ruled out allowing some students to go to the gymnastics corner before the track, even though the effort of keeping them on the track took a lot of our time and attention. I talked to the paras about the best way to do this and asked them to do nothing but use their body position to contain students and keep them out of the gymnastics corner while I led the warmup. It was a bit odd to see the paras standing at a distance like guards when they normally interacted so closely with students, but that proved to be the most effective way to keep the class on task. It wasn't one

FIGURE 8.3 A linear challenge course has an inherent directional flow that students recognize.

hundred percent effective, and there was still some dodging and chasing as three of our seven students darted toward the far corner when they saw an opening. Fran had an idea. Instead of centering the track in the gym, the mat hexagon near one far corner and the gymnastics setup in the other far corner in a giant triangle, could we try compressing everything – making the track smaller and putting everything along one wall? That way there was only an outlet on one side if students chose to elope, and the space would be much easier to manage. For our next class I set up everything as she had suggested, and it helped.

Before trying to manage off-task behavior by putting more adults on the problem, I re-think the environment. Here is what I pay attention to:

- Is there an obvious traffic flow to the space so that students don't have to guess where to go?

- Is one element causing distractions? If so, can I modify or eliminate it?
- What are the paras doing? Have I communicated my goals to them, and can the adults be deployed more effectively?

Given that elopement occurs frequently in Firefly PE, and that it must be addressed so that students remain engaged with learning, I try to utilize walls, corners, and mats so it is easier for adults to contain the space.

Use More Staff or Helping Buddies

Redeploying the adults is a practical way to manage situations. With two adults it's easier to model partner activities like tossing, catching, tagging, and fleeing. But it's also effective to have a peer buddy participate, and students would rather play with peers than adults. Every once in a while the principal or dean brings down a student who has been spending time in the office and would benefit from the opportunity to help a younger student. The effect on the helper is striking. When you offer a student who has been in trouble the option of going to another classroom to help or mentor someone, their reaction is almost always positive. They relish the chance to cast off the old mood of anger and alienation for a fresh start in a new environment where they are viewed as a responsible person, and not a troublemaker. The students they help become the beneficiaries of this positive energy.

The prerequisite for any kind of buddy or peer tutoring to work is to teach it as you would any other important content:

- Ideally, on a day that your student(s) who has special needs is not in class explain that many students have special skills and special challenges.
- Discuss the challenges we personally face and where we sometimes could use a helping hand. Students love to volunteer information about illness, injuries, and life

challenges. If you have created an open and respectful classroom environment, students are eager to jump into this kind of discussion.
- A key inclusion principle is to avoid making an issue of a student's disability or difference. You can't hide or cover it up, but you can create opportunities for *all* students to be helpers as well as recipients. If your new student is going to need a partner to guide them during a game, you can offer the same option to other students who would like buddies. That way, no one stands out.
- Describe some of the challenges that their new classmate is likely to face. Ask for their ideas.
- Once you have an acceptable list of ways that your students are ready to help, discuss the buddy schedule. Everyone needs to be clear that it will ultimately be up to your new student(s) to accept help.

Reduce the Distance between Players; Bring Play Closer to the Ground

These strategies for minimizing play stoppages are familiar to coaches and PE teachers. Reducing the distance between players immediately increases the accuracy of throws and reduces the incidence of dropped balls. Bringing play closer to the ground has a similar effect, and both strategies can be adopted by the players without any help from adults, assuming the teacher has taken the time to practice and reinforce it. As obvious as these adaptations may appear to the average person, it takes some maturity before children use them on their own. I've also noticed a gender difference. Elementary school boys tend to put up with a lot of bad throws and missed catches if they can chuck the ball far. Girls tend to be a little more conservative and place more value on completing passes and catches. In any case, I often use this strategy with the Fireflies. Being so simple, the concepts barely need to be explained. For nonverbal students, I get more physically involved. I use motion gestures, or I will just sit on the floor and practice with them for a while.

Create New Roles

Creating a new role or job within the game to solve a specific issue is a strategy you tend to use as you get more experienced. As you observe your students, you quickly see the weak points in the lesson where play stops, there's down time, or friction develops between students. So, you may select a responsible student to referee, or you may give a capable student the job of "ball chaser." A lesson in which students recognize problems, do the troubleshooting and adopt new roles to facilitate the activity probably says more about the students and the teacher than it does about the lesson design. Especially if it is an elementary grade, that kind of behavior doesn't just happen. You are seeing the result of a lot of deliberate teaching and practice, and in our district, it is one of the prerequisites for receiving a job evaluation of "distinguished" as opposed to "proficient." It is evidence that students are taking responsibility for their own learning. We teachers remind ourselves that "distinguished" is not a place you live, but rather a place you try to visit. The truth is, that kind of teaching takes more planning and patience, but the payoff is worth it.

Before I run into a situation where I know some students will complain and protest that the game is too hard, or they are too tired, or they don't know how to play, I prepare options ahead of time. Inclusion means making sure everyone participates, and no one opts out. That means being ready with a few different tasks related to the main activity but different enough to be appealing to students with various abilities. Take micro soccer for example. Teaching the class how to referee ensures that they learn the rules of the game, and it requires practicing fairness and concentration. A ref cannot stand still, so they will also get some exercise moving up and down the court/field. In micro soccer the fields are small, so balls tend to go out of bounds frequently, so we use ball chasers: one on each sideline and one behind each goal. Have colored vests available so they feel special. A third option we frequently use are skill sharpening drills students can practice off the field, like pass and trap with a buddy.

Instead of one field, I set up three so that I can create games that accommodate my students' skill levels. I may want to group students with similar skills, or I may want to place some highly skilled players with players whose skills are just developing. When doing that, it's important to let those skilled players know that they are not being punished. They are being selected by virtue of their experience to help others who have not had their opportunities. Then I instruct them on ways of coaching and assisting their teammates:

- ♦ Be like a quarterback or a captain.
- ♦ Guide teammates where to go when they are unsure.
- ♦ Make perfect passes.
- ♦ Spread the ball around.
- ♦ Model enthusiasm and good sportsmanship.

If you don't keep notes on your classes, you forget a lot of the "brilliant" ideas that occur to you when you're caught up in the midst of teaching. When I'm in the middle of an activity with students, unforeseen issues always crop up, but changing and adding students' roles and responsibilities is usually *not* the first thing to occur to me when I'm in problem-solving mode. That is something that is better planned rather than done on the fly. It will take time to explain, teach, model and practice.

Break the Lesson Down into Pieces

Let's say that you decide that it's worth taking the time to introduce the concept of chasing down a runaway ball because it's essential in any kind of ballgame. If your students' play skills are still in the developing stage, you can't treat the idea of ball chasing as something that's obvious. When you're teaching students who have immigrated from other countries or have certain disabilities, you find that there is more that cannot be taken for granted. How are you going to go about it? You can try the model>demonstrate>practice technique. Your paras can help you demonstrate, then substitute a few of your most capable students, then divide into a couple of groups, or you can divide the skill into its components and teach each one in sequence to the whole class. There is no right or wrong here. Because the skill range in my Firefly class is so wide and is weighted toward the middle-bottom, I need to skew my teaching that way. Even though "ball chasing" is a single concept, it's not a single skill, and we try to identify and isolate each skill component before practicing it, so we have more success.

You might decide that ball retrieval is a not-too-distant cousin of "cleanup." Since your students are already very familiar with the cleanup process, you may be able to start with that angle. Equipment is out of place – we must get it and put it where it belongs. We can spread a bunch of rubber animals, beanbags and yarn balls around the gym, and then, on a signal, we cleanup/pick up the objects and sort them in different buckets. We can gradually move the buckets further from the objects to challenge their endurance and attention. From there we might transition to groups of three, each with one adult, practicing the same activity. With cleanup/retrieval or whatever you want to call it, under their belts, your students have learned an important routine that you can generalize to other situations. When I have **multi-step directions** for students to follow, I am much more inclined to just say, "Follow me." It's a lot easier and quicker than telling them what to do. With multi-step directions, students typically jump up when the first one is barely out of my mouth. If I am going to relay multiple directions, I start off by telling them how many directions there will be in total and to wait till I say "GO." Even though I have two or three paras supporting the Firefly class, I still preview the steps out loud, and that gives the paras a heads-up too.

Think about It Questions

You plan to have your fourth graders play Sharks and Minnows the next time they come to PE. However, you have some concerns about Jenny. Based on experience, you know that she does not like tag games. She is fearful of the commotion and contact. Refer to the chapter and select one or more strategies that might help Jenny participate. Describe how you would implement them.

List as many games as you can think of that would be more inclusive for diverse abilities by utilizing the strategy of reducing distance between players and/or bringing play closer to the ground.

You have been observing students at recess and notice that several students always watch their classmates playing kickball but never participate. Describe how you might help them get involved. How could you use some of their PE time to accomplish this?

You have a gen. ed. PE class that is doing a parachute lesson. One of your students, "Aaron," is autistic and nonverbal. He tends not to interact with others, and his behavior can be very disruptive. Aaron is accompanied by a newly hired paraeducator who is inexperienced and looking to you for guidance. There is a lot of energy and noise as the class performs various maneuvers with the parachute. When they attempt to make a "mushroom mountain" by raising the chute and quickly lowering it so that it inflates, Aaron crawls onto the chute and lies down in the middle. The activity comes to a halt. Choose one of the following approaches and outline a plan that specifies roles for Aaron, the paraeducator, the other students, and you, the teacher.

1. Allow Aaron to stay on the parachute and incorporate him into the activity. Since you have more than one parachute, you are able to create a second or third group.
2. Require Aaron to get off the parachute using the least amount of hands-on prompting necessary and give him a spot between two helpful buddies.
3. You decide that the parachute may be too advanced a concept for Aaron, and you believe you can incorporate some of the same goals (cooperation, object manipulation) using different equipment.

9

Curriculum, Lesson Design, Scope, and Sequence

My guiding principles for teaching all students are:

- to be physically active in class
- to learn skills and gain knowledge that will help them lead an active and healthy life
- to have fun

The road that each student takes in pursuit of these principles is unique. Some travel independently once given some direction while others need continual guidance and support.

Interplay between Standards, Units, and SMART Goals: Jump Rope and Challenge Course

While the PE teachers at all sixteen of our elementary schools use the same curriculum as well as SHAPE America National Standards, we choose the units we teach, design our own lessons, and sequence them. I enjoy the balance we have between

FIGURE 9.1 It's more fun to shoot at a regulation basket, but it requires a safe, stable platform for younger students.

a body of shared resources and the freedom to implement our programs as we see fit. It allows me to be inventive and to design a program that works for my school and my students. I recognize that when we are starting out in the profession, we rely heavily on advice and lesson plans that our colleagues share, but as we gain experience, we tend to follow our own paths with more confidence while remaining true to standards and policies.

Because we are constantly collaborating, there is a lot of similarity between our programs. The district requires this continuity so that if students change schools, they are not caught off-guard. Some units are favored by several PE teachers but not by others. However, our team is virtually unanimous in including a jump rope unit in our curricula. The reason is clear when one sees that jump rope is given its own category under motor skills and checks off all five SHAPE national standards plus all six skill-related fitness components:

SHAPE National Standards:
- Standard 1: The physically literate individual demonstrates competency in a variety of motor skills and movement patterns.
- Standard 2: The physically literate individual applies knowledge of concepts principles, strategies, and tactics related to movement and performance.
- Standard 3: The physically literate individual demonstrates the knowledge and skills to achieve and maintain a health-enhancing level of physical activity and fitness.
- Standard 4: The physically literate individual exhibits responsible personal and social behavior that respects self and others.
- Standard 5: The physically literate individual recognizes the value of physical activity for health, enjoyment, challenge, self-expression, and/or social interaction.

Health-Related Fitness Components (Cowan et al. 2013):
- Cardiorespiratory endurance
- Muscle endurance

Six Skill-Related Fitness Components (Pangrazi 2004):
- Balance
- Agility
- Speed
- Power
- Coordination
- Reaction time

I would also add cross-cultural appeal and cost as important benefits. Jump rope is practiced all over the world with a wonderful variety of styles and expressions. The sport is low-cost, requires no specialized equipment, court, or field, and can be performed indoors or outdoors. These are features that ensure equity and access.

On average, 50% of my fifth graders exhibit basic jump rope proficiency. Very few have advanced skills like double under, crossover or can-can. The beauty of a jump rope unit is that most of the class will attain several advanced steps and be able to put together a 20–30-second performance by the end of a 4-week unit. Lesson sequence may change from year to year but always builds skill upon skill while offering many opportunities for independent practice and peer collaboration. The number of jump rope activities in one class period depends on concurrent units we must make time for. Except on performance days, jump rope is usually one of several different activities in a class period. This is a typical lesson sequence.

TABLE 9.1 Unit/Lesson Sequence: Jump Rope

Unit: Jump Rope Skills, Practice and Performance
SHAPE K-12 Standards:
Standard 1. Demonstrate competency in a variety of motor skills and movement patterns>Manipulative>Jump Rope(S1.E27)
APENS:
Standard 7. Curriculum Theory and Development>Understand how to plan a sequence of learning experiences that lead to the achievement of specified goals or learning outcomes>Plan for program goals that are specifically designed to meet the long-term fitness, motor skills, physical activity, and recreational needs of individuals with disabilities and reflect the family and community values.

Student Behaviors	Teacher behaviors	Time Mins
Seated at Home Base	Demonstrates procedure for taking rope from rack and replacing it. Examples of inappropriate behavior (yanking rope so that several fall off) and courteous behavior.	5
After warmup laps, students choose a rope from the rack, find a personal space and practice independently.	Instructions on whiteboard at entrance inform class that they will get a jump rope after 3-minute jog and chat warmup. Observe by walking around the gym, giving attention to individual students.	5–10
View jump rope videos that highlight basic and advanced jump rope steps.	Pause video occasionally to explain or answer questions. Pause after each step for short demonstrations.	10
Refer to cards and practice a different step at each station.	Set up jump rope station rotation with cards illustrating different steps. Choose one or two stations for focused observation.	15

(Continued)

TABLE 9.1 (Continued)

Stand on personal exercise spots[a] with a jump rope. Practice while watching the video projection.	Project videos on wall. Practice with the students.	10
Show me their progress in the performance zone when they are ready.	Set up a square near your teaching area with cones. A chair and a clipboard allow you to take notes for students and be comfortable. It also shows students that you are completely focused on them so they will tend to give their best effort.	10–15
Students who prove mastery of steps coach their peers. Students may request a coach.	Explain how coaching works.	5
Seated at Home Base or around the learning circle with a copy of the rubric.	Explain the jump rope performance rubric, how to use it, and scoring categories.	10
Return to independent practice with jump rope rubric and begin outlining their performance routine using template with word bank listing jumping steps.	Circulate throughout gym. Short observation and chat with every student. Remind students that there is a written element of the performance. They earn points for completing all required template elements and for legibility.	
Sign up for performance time slots on whiteboard. Class discussion on performance and audience behavior.	Answer questions.	10
Last 2 classes of jump rope unit: When it's their turn to perform, student hands me their completed template listing the steps and number of repetitions. Rest of class exhibits appropriate audience behavior.	Practice/performance zone has remained in place throughout the unit so that students are accustomed to it. Use their template to score performance.	25
Short post-performance conference with teacher.	Review and discuss scores you have assigned for each requirement of the rubric.	1

(Continued)

TABLE 9.1 (Continued)

OPTION: After performances, students may volunteer to perform with a partner in front of the class with music accompaniment.	This is a fun culminating activity.	10–15
OPTION: Some older students may volunteer to perform during lunch or an assembly.	Get permissions and schedule this with front office.	10

a Personal Exercise spots mirror our Home Base order. Spots are in rows and columns and spaced far enough apart for students to jump rope without collision. Use flat markers like poly spots, or draw dots on the floor, or if you are fortunate to be involved in remodel/reflooring plans, make sure that these are a feature of your new floor. Different colors for the rows are helpful.

The process for aligning my units with standards is straightforward. I look at our curriculum units first, and then I refer to the standards descriptors and grade-level outcomes when designing lessons to make sure I cover the essential learnings and am not leaving out something important. For Example, the **SHAPE national standards** grade-level outcomes that apply to my challenge course unit are easy to locate. Under Standard 1, motor skills and movement patterns, grade 3, there are three subheadings: **Locomotor, Nonlocomotor, and Manipulative**. Under **Locomotor**, there are three relevant subsections:

- Jumping & Landing, Horizontal (S1.E3) The descriptor is "Jumps and lands in the horizontal plane using a mature pattern."
- Jumping & Landing, Vertical (S1.E4) The descriptor is "Jumps and lands in the vertical plane using a mature pattern."
- Combinations (S1.E6) The descriptor is "Performs a sequence of locomotor skills, transitioning from one skill to another smoothly and without hesitation."

Under **Nonlocomotor (stability)**, four grade level outcomes are relevant. The outcomes and third grade descriptors are:

- Balance (S1.E7) "Balances on different bases of support, demonstrating muscular tension and extensions of free body parts."
- Weight transfer (S1.E8) "Transfers weight from feet to hands for momentary weight support."
- Weight transfer, rolling (S1.E9) "Applies skill."
- Curling & stretching, twisting & bending (S1.E10) "Moves into and out of gymnastics balances with curling, twisting & stretching actions."

SHAPE's **Critical Elements** for grades K-5 (pages 18–25) describe and illustrate the locomotor and manipulative skills but for some reason leave out the non-locomotor skills.

Challenge/gymnastics courses are unique in their applicability to certain **APENS adapted PE standards**. The components that have to do with the **vestibular** (apparatus in the inner ear that provides signals related to movement in space) and **proprioceptive** (the body's sensory information that results in the sense of position and movement) systems under **Standard 2 Motor Behavior** are relevant since my students exhibit a lot of diversity in those areas.

- Component 2.01.04.01 "Understand typical sensory development related to the visual, auditory, tactile, vestibular, and proprioceptive systems > Develop and implement programs that strengthen orthoptic (related to the muscles that enable eye movement) visual abilities such as visual fixation, pursuit, and search behaviors."
- Component 2.01.04.03 "Understand common deviations in the development of the tactile system among individuals with disabilities > Develop and implement programs to enhance individuals' abilities to tolerate various levels of tactile stimuli."
- Component 2.01.04.04 "Understand common deviations in the development of the vestibular system among individuals with disabilities > Select and design activities to help remediate balance problems related to vestibular functioning."

- Component 2.01.06.01 "Understand the significance of development delays throughout the lifespan on balance and related tasks > Develop and implement programs that stimulate vestibular, visual, and proprioceptive senses."

As I plan instruction, it is helpful to think of the big ideas that I want all students to learn. These can be macro goals:

- Improve muscle strength.
- Develop skills for recreational activities like soccer or volleyball.
- Develop skills for social interaction, sports, and recreation such as going to a health club or public pool or learning the skills for being a teammate.

Then I'll analyze those for the required short-term objectives describing specific instructional targets. These are also known as SMART goals – Specific, Measurable, Achievable, Realistic, and Time frame (Grenier 2014, p. 15). The student–teacher and student-to-student discussions about goal setting are invaluable. It is the ideal way to clarify thinking and arrive at smart goals. These are a few examples of smart goals:

- Learn to hold a racket with correct form and strike a ball.
- Learn three different ways to use a dumbbell.
- Identify equipment and clothing for a softball game.
- Walk down a 10-foot balance beam without stepping off.
- Perform a basic jump rope action.

With goals and targets identified, students can demonstrate performance by different means according to their ability. The time frame can be specific, e.g., by end of the semester, or can remain flexible. With some students the time frame is open-ended. We practice skills for as long as we need to, modify the conditions as necessary, and measure the improvement. The benchmarks and expectations are obviously different at different grade levels and for any student who has an IEP. There is a wide range of expectations for jump rope:

- Be able to sustain a 15-second performance using one basic and one advanced step.
- Be able to perform five consecutive jumps using the basic or double-bounce step.
- Be able to hold rope correctly, flip it overhead, step across.
- Lay rope on floor in straight line or circle and jump back and forth, in and out.
- Walk across rope.

It often requires a lot of trial and error before I arrive at a lesson design that reflects my gen. ed. curriculum and is also suitable for my students who have impactful disabilities. I never want to relegate my students who have special needs to a separate educational track from my neurotypical students. The gen. ed. curriculum and the Firefly curriculum are like two vehicles on a road, each travelling at its own speed and taking detours along the way. Keeping them together is not always possible, but they should meet up periodically.

Assessment & Measuring Growth

Sometimes it is difficult to measure growth with students who have severe intellectual or physical disabilities. Patrick and a few other students were unable to propel themselves on a 4-wheel scooter even with adaptations like the suspended rope. It is possible that when I saw "failure" with some of the things I tried, there were signs of learning that I was missing. Maybe if I had thought to measure "time balanced on scooter while being towed" as evidence of improvement, I could have created an assessable learning opportunity. Students with restricted mobility who may also be nonverbal communicators still have to be assessed. You will use the same tools that you use with other students to figure out what to do:

- Identify an important behavior.
- Break it down into measurable components.
- Teach it and practice it multiple times.
- Look for progress.

What would assessment look like for a student like Patrick with multiple challenges or even a student who remains in a wheelchair? It is not all that complicated. What are the tasks and equipment that I have given them? Think **duration** and/or **frequency**. I can measure amount of time holding an object of a certain weight, amount of time shaking a can full of paperclips, or number of hand-passes to a buddy. What are the measurables that a student's parents, physical therapist, or doctor looks for that indicate improving health? Those might give you some ideas. Assessable learning comes in many forms. I remember commenting to Chandra one day that Patrick's shirt wasn't as wet as it normally was. She said that they had had some success getting him to chew on a fidget rather than his shirt. That is an example of effective teaching as well as measurable learning. As I mentioned earlier, focus and attention are challenges for some students, and they are key elements of success. If that is the case, then they should be assessed. For Patrick, we measured several key learnings:

- Amount of time spent in the instructional area before eloping
- Number of repetitions of a task such as step-ups, hand passes, ball rolls
- Amount of time able to sit on a balance ball
- Instances of cooperation with adults and classmates such as carrying equipment
- Instances of travelling to the correct target location

There are multiple opportunities for assessment of performance on even a simple challenge course. Imagine the possibilities when you include an incline wedge, a trapezoid, a balance beam, or a cylinder. Each one of these features is a potential assessment point. I found that I had to focus all my attention on one section of the course at a time to assess my students properly. Take the small plastic slide for example. We placed it in a challenge course loop after a step box and before the mini trampoline. At first glance it appears that there are three tasks: climb the steps, go down the slide, then exit onto the trampoline. In fact, I'm watching for about five distinct behaviors:

1. Wait on step box when someone else is on the slide.
2. Climb 3 steps to top of slide.
3. Maneuver legs and feet from steps to sitting position at top of slide.
4. Go down slide.
5. Stand and step onto the trampoline.

It wasn't until I had the opportunity to watch a substitute teacher teach my own PE class that my eyes really opened to the assessment opportunities for even my most impacted students. The longer I observed, the more I recognized behaviors that could be assessed, regardless of students' abilities. Because the two are so intertwined, it was obvious that recording teacher behavior side by side with student behavior would provide valuable feedback. There is potential for data measurement in all phases of a class from warmup, direct instruction, seat time, and game to cleanup and lineup. Discrete behaviors can be measured in terms of frequency and/or duration.

- Elapsed time before student leaves their preferred location and joins the activity.
- Frequency of leaving preferred location and joining activity. Of these, how many required adult guidance?
- Frequency of elopements.
- Duration of elopements.
- Duration of time in instructional area.
- Duration of time in instructional area participating appropriately. With and without adult support.
- Frequency of attention/eye focus on teacher/peers.
- Frequency initiating positive/negative interactions.
- Frequency of redirection by teacher or paraeducator.
- Frequency of student appropriately requesting a sensory break.

Behaviors that Promote Learning is one of two subsections in our report card, the other being **Skills and Concepts**. There are seven key behaviors: **respect, responsibility, collaboration, persistence, flexibility, problem solving, speaking and listening** – each of which is broken down into descriptors. These concepts are general enough to be adapted for all students. While I have different expectations for different students, some expectations apply to everyone. For example, when we are gathered on the learning circle to practice muscle-strengthening exercises with resistance tubes, everyone must be in location on or near a poly spot and have eyes on the teacher. Maintaining attention in an academic environment always involves an element of persistence. Ability to attend is a cornerstone of learning. For some students, proximity among their classmates meets this expectation.

Maybe one reason that Patrick did not play with balls or pull ropes was that he preferred to watch us. To him, we were much more interesting than things. I believe that my approach to him was misguided at times. Many of my efforts had to do with *mechanics*: To find a ball he would throw; to find a weight he would lift or push; to modify a scooter that he could ride. While Patrick's IEP specified a specially designed PE class, periodic inclusion in gen. ed. with peers who assisted him might have been a catalyst to expand learning. His enjoyment of peers and sense of wonderment coupled with a preferred activity such as a challenge course could have provided the foundation for a more varied PE experience. As I stated at the beginning, having an inventor's mindset, the habit of reflection, a willingness to accept mistakes and the patience to try many things are central to my professional journey. Instead of trying over and over to get him to do things he didn't want to do or couldn't do, and applying my health and fitness standards to him, I could have altered course. No matter how I made him struggle to do this or that task, he was always happy when I worked with him. He communicated in the way he knew how. It is only in hindsight that I realize what a positive young man Patrick was and how he reinforced my belief that **relationship is primary**.

Think about It Questions

An IEP typically includes goals in these areas: cognitive, social/emotional, and adaptive. Each may contain specific objectives and benchmarks. Review the IEP for one of your students. Choose a subsection and draft corresponding objectives and benchmarks for PE. Share your draft with someone on the IEP team such as a special education teacher or physical therapist.

Describe an instance where you adapted equipment for a student who had a disability or provided them with an alternative that allowed them to be successful. Describe the steps or events that led up to your adaptation. Describe the student's experience with the equipment. What were your thoughts afterwards?

The next time you set up a challenge/tumbling course, do so with specific objectives for different areas and pieces of equipment. For example,

- Balance endurance
- Flexibility
- Leaping and landing
- Core strength
- Turn-taking
- Agility
- Rolling

Next, choose an area in the course or a piece of equipment for assessing one of your objectives.

I admit that my approach to Patrick was misguided in some sense due to my focus on mechanics at the expense of really getting to know him and thus working with his strengths (social). In what way are these shortcomings significant? Do they signify that uncertainty is a part of teaching no matter how experienced you are? Is there a natural "lifecycle" to the job of teaching? Could you describe it as a curve? Does that curve go steadily upward, or are there occasional dips? Sketch your teaching "lifecycle" on a piece of paper. Indicate important events on the curve. Make sure to include downs as well as ups!

Put on your "parent hat" and reflect on your own children, nieces, or nephews. Are there any social, behavioral, or play skills that you wish a PE teacher could have worked on with them? For example, did your son turn off to competitive games because they made him nervous and stressed? Did your daughter become disappointed with herself anytime she didn't meet her own expectations? Did your nephew's autism and tendency to insist on a favorite ball, color or position make cooperative play difficult? How would you address some of these issues in the classroom or gym?

10

Collaborating to Meet Challenges

Being a Special Educator

The room 407 staff is comprised of the certificated special ed. teacher and a team of well-trained and experienced paraeducators. Others who are an integral part of the team and frequently rotate in on a scheduled basis are the speech language pathologist, the occupational therapist, the physical therapist, and the school psychologist. They may work with students inside room 407 or they may take them to their own offices. The principal and counselor may also be frequent attendees, but that depends on how their duties are defined and on what is required to work with and support students effectively. I've noticed that some principals are constantly helping in the special education classrooms, while others do so much less frequently. I have a feeling that some principals just have more of an affinity for working in that classroom. It's not that they "like" the 407 students and staff more, but that they have the training and experience that allow them to be comfortable there and to feel like they are an effective support. Only four of the sixteen elementary schools in my district have LRC II programs, and therefore it is possible to be a teacher or administrator in our district for your whole career without having regular contact with students who have very challenging physical, mental, and emotional disabilities. For those of us who do have the opportunity, we are rewarded professionally and personally. We benefit from the special skills we acquire and from the relationships we form.

Room 407 is a very pleasant space. It is two classrooms joined but divided into zones, each with its own purpose and function. Aside from some shelves, tables, and a couple of five-foot room dividers for quiet areas, the space is entirely open. Students are usually spread out working alone or with a para assisting them. The atmosphere is relaxed. I stop in at least once a week for various reasons. Sometimes it's to let them know that I will be taking the class outside for PE. Sometimes it's to confer about a student, or to ask Camille her thoughts about an activity I'm planning. Or it might be to borrow or loan a piece of equipment. It is a place where I always feel welcomed and never made to feel that I am interrupting. As a fellow special educator, we are on the same team in a very real sense. We share the same students, but we also share the recognition that we are *advocates* as well as teachers.

Special education teachers struggle at times to feel as though they are equally part of the staff. The fact is that they don't participate fully in the social life of the school as other teachers do. The main reason is that with their student population, they are always on call. They never have the luxury of taking an undisturbed half-hour lunch break in the staffroom. They also have an enormous administrative workload that is foreign to regular classroom teachers and is dictated by federal and state law and by district regulations. Given that they are always "on call," breaks or no breaks, it's clear why special education teachers are unable to participate in all events, meetings, and conversations that occur among staff throughout the day. I'm sure this is a big reason why they sometimes feel isolated and why they appreciate interaction with coworkers.

I can't remember the reason I was going down to room 407 to talk to Camille. When I looked through the window, I could see that there was no one in the room with her except for the SLP, so I opened the door. It was probably during lunch. Camille waved me in, so I let the door close behind me and waited there. I saw that the two of them were engaged in a serious conversation. They were talking in very low voices, and my sense was that the subject was serious and had to do with events that were unfolding. She gestured toward the phone and seemed to be referring to someone she had just spoken to. After a couple of minutes, the SLP left, and Camille turned to me. "Just another day in paradise," she said with an ironic smile. "This is the fourth time today I've been on the phone with CPS (Child Protective Services)." I think I murmured something like, "Oh no." She turned to look at me.

> Remember that safety plan we have for Gemma? We need to rev it up. There are new court orders in place. I just talked to her caseworker. I'm going to need to meet with you and all of Gemma's teachers again to share the new plan for keeping her safe while she's at school.

I had known that a certain member of Gemma's household was not allowed on school premises. All staff members that needed to be aware of this, had a photo of the person as a reminder, but it had been many months since the notification, and I had not given it much thought recently.

What do you do after you have just learned disturbing information about abuse or neglect of one of your students? The first issue is safety, and you focus immediately on your role and responsibilities within the school's plan. But at the same time, you can't help but reflect on the human factor. While you feel the emotions, you are buoyed by the fact that you are part of a team, and that the burden will be shared. In an opinion piece in the *Washington Post* Danielle Allen and Ashish Jha advocated for keeping schools open during the coronavirus pandemic, citing the essential role they play in the lives of students who are at risk: "Schools are a refuge from a precarious home life, a place where observant teachers can be a safety net." Teachers know that home life for some portion of our students is indeed "precarious" and that, by contrast, the stability school provides is a social and emotional support that is as important as reading, writing and math.

I wondered how Camille faced the emotions. I only saw Gemma for an hour a week, but she spent hours a day in Camille's classroom. How do you keep it together and continue doing your job while dealing with these issues? I'm not surprised that the HR postings for special education teachers are a yard long and only seem to grow as the year progresses. Between the myriad reports and meetings required by law, the extraordinary demands of teaching students who need to be physically managed at times as well as the emotional stamina required to constantly advocate for equitable treatment of your students – it's no wonder that the job turnover rate in room 407 is higher than for any other position in the school. When you have a teacher in that room who is good at their job, you better treat them like the Queen of England.

While there are some regular classroom teachers who like having students with disabilities assigned to their classroom for certain periods and subjects (inclusion), others are wary. They look at it as more planning, more paperwork, more meetings, plus the challenge of having to explain behavior to their other students. That drives Camille nuts. In her mind, even allowing for periods of unregulated behavior, there is no downside to including students with special needs in gen. ed. classes. The benefits to neurotypical students, as well as those who have disabilities, far outweigh any inconveniences. I have known teachers who said that they did not feel prepared to take on students with special needs. A combination of coursework and/or training, mentorship and experience is all that is needed.

As an ELL instructor and program director, I ran up against this dynamic often. In a school district with over 1,400 teachers, fewer than five had an ELL teacher's endorsement or certification. I don't blame the district for this lack. We were not Chicago or Los Angeles. Growth in our population of students who were not native English speakers was accelerating faster than our ability to create the infrastructure to accommodate it. It was my responsibility to provide support and training to gen. ed. teachers when they had ELL students. There were a couple of principals who understood the importance of providing the necessary training to their staff and would invite me to do in-service training. However, most of the time I was a little like an on-call physician. I would get a call or email from a teacher asking for help. Sometimes it was when they received their first ELL student. Other times it was when an ELL student had been in their class for a few weeks, and they realized they didn't have the tools to work with them. I loved this part of my job. Basically, all I did was 1. recognize the difficulty of their situation and sympathize 2. provide them with a little background on language acquisition and cultural differences 3. demonstrate how to use the teaching materials that I would leave with them. That was enough to get them on their feet and to feel some confidence. Ironically, there were several cases when a teacher acquired experience and expertise teaching ELL students, and then the following year none were placed in their class! They were frustrated that they had developed this confidence and then were no longer able to build on it. I told them, "Yes and no." They should use their ELL teaching skills with their native speakers, and it would help them too. The same dynamic applies with the skills I have gained working with students who have special needs. The communication and inclusion strategies I have developed have helped me with all of my students.

Not collaborating with the human resources you have in your own building is a HUGE missed opportunity. If you are a gen. ed. PE teacher, you may have had very little professional development around adapted physical education. I know I didn't. Help arrived in two ways: 1. experience and 2. collaboration with those on my staff who knew my students best. Each person brings their unique expertise and point of view, and during my career I have learned so much from each of them. Collaboration time between Specialists (PE teacher, music teacher, librarian, ELL teacher, Reading Specialist, Social Emotional Health Specialist, and Instructional Coach) and the Special Education Team was not built into our schedule, so we took the initiative. In addition to the informal conversations around students and methods, we arranged with the principal for collaboration time for our two teams when staff meetings and workshops were geared to the K-5 classroom teachers.

These are the school collaborators with whom I work closely to benefit our students with special needs:

TABLE 10.1 Professional Collaborators and Topics

Title	Areas of Collaboration
Special Education classroom teachers	IEP goals, curriculum planning, student background related to abilities, unexpected behavior, illness, family, sensory issues, communication modalities and technology, inclusion.
Special Education paraeducators	Teaching strategies and lesson sequence, students' current emotional state, antecedents that could affect behavior in PE, teamwork, and roles and responsibilities in PE class.
Physical Therapist	PT goals and benchmarks specified in IEP, in-class real-time assessment, PE teacher's responses to periodic questionnaires about student growth.
Occupational Therapist	OT goals and benchmarks specified in IEP, in-class real-time assessment, PE teacher's responses to periodic questionnaires about student growth.
Speech Language Therapist	Language and communication, programming iPad with PE-related language, visual aids including graphics and pictograms.
School Psychologist	Students who are tested and referred for special education services.
School Counselor	Discussions about behavior of students who do not have IEPs, in-class real-time student observation and support, counselor pull-out support.
Instructional Coach/ Positive Behavior Support Coach	Discussions about behavior of students who do not have IEPs but need additional support, useful teaching strategies and positive student support systems, in-class visits to observe and provide direct support to students by listening and practicing self-calming methods.
School Principal	Discussions about scheduling meeting time with district PE team, collaboration with other schools, administrative initiatives from district office.
Dean of Students	Student conferences regarding behavior.

Parents, Students, and Teachers: A Partnership

The confidentiality and privacy laws respecting public school students are very strict, and even more prescriptive when it comes to any student who has an IEP. The Individuals with

Disabilities Education Act (IDEA) has provisions which specifically protect privacy of students, as well as parents' rights to receive notifications, examine documents and provide consent for sharing of records.[1] Personal and home information about students is restricted. According to federal and state law, all that I am entitled to know about my students' conditions and educational plan is in their IEP and in their FBA (Functional Behavior Assessment) and BIP (Behavior Intervention Plan) in some cases. I receive a copy of the IEP, and I sometimes attend IEP meetings with the students' parents, teachers, and specialists. However, parents do not always share those most personal details that are on the one hand very private and potentially embarrassing but on the other hand quite useful to know in coming to a better understanding of their child. The underlying causes of many students' difficulties can be understood if parents are brave enough and motivated enough to share that information. Put yourself in the parents' shoes, and it's easy to see why this is so difficult. If we, as educators, have earned parents' trust, they are more likely to share information with us.

We create trust with our students' parents by being respectful, empathetic and by doing our job conscientiously. When teachers meet with parents to discuss their children, it's safe to say that we sometimes engage in a certain amount of mental jiu jitsu to avoid appearing callous while trying to have a frank and honest exchange. Most of us are also parents, and we know what it's like to hear painful things about your child from their teacher. We have a policy at our school to begin every parent–teacher meeting with positive remarks. It may take a lot of reflection to come up with a list of positive traits and behaviors for students like Romy and Kayden, especially if you have neglected assessing them. On the other hand, if you have done regular assessments, even for the simplest of skills, then you have a body of information about a student that their parents are usually very happy to hear about. Their child accomplishes things at school that they have never witnessed. You can share anecdotes that won't appear on a report card or IEP that they will only learn of when a teacher relates them.

Our school district has a very diverse population. We are a suburban district with families coming from dozens of nations speaking dozens of languages. Many come for jobs in the tech industry. As diverse as we are, our population of students with special needs has an even higher proportion of international students than the general population. Parents have told us that they come to the US because they are looking for a better education for their children with special needs. Gemma's family had immigrated a few years ago from the Philippines. No doubt they had done research ahead of time and probably had friends and family in the United States. But coming from that distant island nation, they would have had to get used to very different cultural norms. It's fair to say that like many immigrant families, Gemma's parents felt pressure to conform and assimilate. They also probably felt pressure to "fix" the problem so that Gemma and the rest of the family could go on to live the "American Dream." While Gemma's mother had said that her daughter was a big reason they moved to the US, she was not very free with details about Gemma's home life. One of the main objectives in any teacher-parent conference is to discuss how we can work in tandem with parents to benefit their children. For example, if they have a reward system at home that works and does not conflict with any of our policies, we want to employ a similar one at school. If the teacher is trying a new academic or behavior strategy in the classroom, it's important to know how that carries over at home. At the very least, we don't want home and school to be at cross purposes.

The student's parents, their classroom teacher, and support paraprofessionals are the advisors you consult when there are unknowns about a student that may be impacting your ability to work with them. There could be several very good reasons to have a consultation. Your student's parents may have requested to be involved in instructional decisions about their son/daughter. You may have struggled to come up with effective lessons for this student. You might be uncertain whether your plan or actions might be counterproductive. It is time to consult these advisors, particularly when you feel that there could be consequences that are not clear to you.

Window or Iceberg? Shared Insights

Sometime after Kayden graduated to middle school, I had a conversation with Camille about the difficulty of reading certain students' thoughts and emotions. That is one of the challenges with Autism Spectrum Disorder. If expression, gesture, and language are windows through which we see into a person's mind and heart, those windows can be somewhat opaque in children who have ASD. She suggested a different metaphor: an iceberg. She said, "What you see is the part that you have to deal with. It's all you have to go on. But what's under the water is where the answers are." You have no idea what could be triggering behavior. Perhaps she didn't have breakfast that morning. Perhaps he didn't like that his shoes were blue. Perhaps she is reacting to the fact that you remind her of someone. The question is, are there ways to see below the waterline? The answer is a qualified *yes*. The difficulty is that it can be almost impossible to do while you are teaching. It really calls for some collaboration and detective work. The easiest thing is to simply talk to the people who know your student best. Another approach that teachers generally find very helpful is to ask a qualified staff person to observe you teach. They can watch your lesson from the time the students enter the gym – even before they enter – until they leave. While you focus on teaching, they can pay attention to your student. They will watch for signs of disengagement or anxiety. They can record the point at which their behavior changed and went from being productive to problematic. They can watch and listen to your responses and to the whole course of your interactions. By recording detailed observations, they may be able to point you to something that you did that seemed insignificant but may have been part of a pattern that triggered behavior. The parents may even allow you to video the lesson once you have explained your plan.

There is no doubt that some people's vision is just more penetrating. The above/below waterline ratio changes depending on who is observing the iceberg. For example, to Ed and to all of Kayden's important adults, that iceberg floated higher than to the rest of us. Here is an example of finally seeing "below the waterline" but, unfortunately, several years after Kayden graduated.

Remember the finger game you learned as a child? "Here is the church, here is the steeple, open the church, see all the people!" This is why I'm reminded of it…

In the classroom they had been teaching Kayden that his learning posture – not quite an "at attention" position and not quite an "at ease" position but somewhere in between – was to be seated at his table, 'feet on floor, hands folded, eyes on teacher' – in those exact words, in that exact order. Each one of these postural elements was important. They ensured that Kayden was able to work and remain in his own personal space. What you saw was a serious-looking young man sitting quietly and alertly. However, as we know, that was the part of the iceberg that lay above the waterline. What you were not seeing was that Kayden may not have wanted to be sitting at that table. He may have been suppressing some discomfort, and if you looked closely, there was one place where that discomfort was visible: his hands. They were neither relaxed nor still. They were in the "church and steeple" position. He was clenching and unclenching. You could see his index fingers flexing, and the pressure was visible as blood was displaced to his fingertips.

At the time, I had no idea, that this had any significance, although I clearly remember the behavior. It's only years later after thinking about it and talking with Camille that I am wondering what that might have signified. Is it possible that if I had paid closer attention to areas of Kayden's face or body that were clenching, like his hands, I might have been better able to sense his mood? Was he in a relaxed, alert state ready to engage, or was he on edge and needed a sensory break option? **Talk to your student's other teachers, and particularly to the paras that support them about the cues they look for indicating relaxed, alert posture or possible behavior escalation.**

Think about It Questions

Think about the times that a student with disabilities was placed in your class. What were your reactions? Do you agree with Camille that there is no downside to including students who have

ASD, intellectual and health disabilities in gen. ed. classrooms? If you don't agree, try to explain the difference in your perspectives. Discuss your answers with a special education teacher.

How often do you talk to the special education teachers in your school? Do you know their names? Have you ever had lunch together? Describe your interactions with them.

Do you think that it was a good idea for Camille to reveal information about Gemma's background? How curious are you about your students' home lives? What kinds of information do you think you are entitled to know? What do you think should remain private? What kind of information about your students' backgrounds is helpful to you as a teacher?

The parents of one of your students do not share information about medical conditions or conditions at home that impact their son/daughter's ability to learn, are there other places where you can legitimately acquire that information?

Note

1 You can read these on the IDEA website, sites.ed.gov/idea/in the sections on Parents' Rights and Procedural Safeguards, sections 1415 and 1439.

11

Looking Forward

Start with the Child

I find that teaching PE for students with special needs is more difficult than teaching gen. ed. PE. To put it as simply as I can, it's just harder to know what to do. The familiar progressions and patterns that I rely on with my neurotypical students become a little fuzzy with my students who have disabilities. Every lesson plan begins with analysis of my students. If I plan an activity, I might decide to scrap it when I realize what will be involved in adapting for students X, Y, and Z. That is not the case with gen. ed. In gen. ed. I differentiate for the range of abilities. I build in challenge options for students who master the skills and tasks early, and I build in scaffolded options for students whose skills are developing. But that is just part of normal teaching. Often you can address those differences in the way you group students by placing one or two more skilled students in each group.

The Firefly lessons I felt best about were usually the products of a lot of trial, error, and modification. The resistance tube process with Romy's class, recognizing limits and learning to be clear with Kayden, the paddle tether with Gemma, the mat hexagon routine for groupwork, the various wheeled attempts with Patrick – these were waypoints in a journey. Anyone who thinks they can follow a roadmap for teaching students who have disabilities like those I've described is in for a surprise. If I were to apprentice in a self-contained special education classroom, I would want to be able to watch and listen for a week without having any tasks. I would also want to be able to sit down with my mentor a couple of times a day and ask questions. If I were the mentor, I would make the apprentice guess at the answers before I gave them my opinions so that I empowered them to take ownership of the process and trust their own thinking.

Recognizing that you must start with an understanding of the student before you know what and how to teach, it's logical that your understanding does not happen all at once, but little by little. Therefore, your lesson design and teaching methods are like putting one brick on top of another. Sometimes the bricks fit, and sometimes they don't. You can create or borrow a plan that's as detailed as you want. You just need to be prepared to backtrack and go in a different direction. A plan doesn't have to be rigid. Think of it as adapting rather than improvising. For example, in the tossing and catching unit, I got part-way through my plan and realized that we would have to detour to one or more lessons on ball retrieval. For Kayden, I would have to proceed more slowly and work with his teacher and para to learn to recognize when we'd reached his limit. We would have to take any type of basketball practice step by step to make sure he was comfortable with the levels of noise, movement, and contact before fully including him. If you want students to experience confidence and mastery, you can't avoid this evaluative process, and there aren't any shortcuts. You pursue the objectives specified in your students' IEPs and in your health and fitness standards, but how you get there can be a long, winding, inventive and mysterious process.

Sometimes when I'd been working with a student for months or even years, and I hit a roadblock with them, I'd ask their classroom teacher to remind me what their diagnoses were – as if that might provide the missing bit of information I needed in order to figure out how to teach them. It never resulted in a lightbulb switching on. There are some obvious exceptions. The IEP will tell you if a student has physical conditions that impact learning, such as hearing and vision loss or a heart condition that requires them to rest frequently. You must be aware of health information pertaining to your students so that you can keep them safe.

Occasionally, a health condition will be revealed or will develop later during the year, and as a PE teacher you may be one of the first adults to suspect a problem, and your response could be critical. A need for frequent rest, frequent drinks, frequent bathroom trips, difficulty maintaining balance – these are things we notice. Knowing that someone had an intellectual disability that gave them the cognitive age of a three-year-old did not provide me with a roadmap for what to do. Knowledge is never a bad thing, but I would tell myself that my job is not to diagnose or provide therapy. Aside from reminding me that learning would be a very incremental process and that the impatience I experienced was to be expected, the awareness of their diagnosis just reinforced the obvious: students learn at different rates and in different ways. The same principles always seem to apply year after year:

- Observe closely.
- Establish rapport.
- Avoid rigidity and be adaptable.
- Embrace clarity in your instruction.
- Trial-error-modification is a dependable strategy.
- Ask questions of those who know your students best.
- PE must teach skills and knowledge, but it also has to be fun.

Successes and Failures

Over the years, I have concluded that how a society treats those with special needs is a measure of how civilized it is. Our school has always been committed to including all our students in all aspects of school life. The extent to which all are included, accepted, and cared for shows especially in the way our students treat each other. Students and staff are accustomed to seeing and hearing unexpected behavior, and they take it in their stride. As a PE program, we have also had successes. We have learned to take kids as they are. We maintain high expectations for all. We have grown our professional knowledge. We include our students in gen. ed. classes as soon as we can, but, more importantly, we pay close attention to their individual needs and try to meet them – wherever that may be. We have finally begun to collaborate more regularly with our colleagues. As a school, we have achieved some successes for our students with special needs. Due to the challenging nature of teaching students with disabilities, it is a good idea to think about how teachers are supported and how we grow professionally. Are we getting the training we need? Are we able to collaborate in a systematic way with colleagues around students' needs? Does our school encourage staff to take initiative with new ideas? Does our school nurture and maintain a culture of "invention?"

If it weren't for the fact that in my own classroom or gym I am the boss, and I have a lot of autonomy, I would feel oppressed by the layers of bureaucracy that I operate under. Public education comes under state authority, and therefore most of the laws governing what we do and how we are compensated are subject to legislation. There is also a constant downstream flow of initiatives coming from our school district administration. Teachers feel that they are barely keeping up with changes, and if you consider *every* job responsibility that is added to the workload, for the most part we are not. So, it isn't surprising that even when we are asked to think outside the box, we don't get past the reality that there aren't enough hours in the day to do what is already required of us, let alone something brand new.

Here is an example of what was lost because we didn't have the time/bandwidth or didn't make it a priority. I'll go out on a limb and say that it was the biggest shortcoming and most serious failure of our special education program: We didn't bring the stakeholders together regularly to collaborate around our students, outside of IEP meetings. An IEP meeting is a unique animal. It's required by law, who must attend is clearly stipulated, and the agenda is rigid. I once counted thirteen people at an IEP meeting: the mother and father of the student plus *eleven* school personnel. I will spare you the tedium of the details. They were all pertinent, all required, all relevant. What you *can't* do in an IEP meeting, even though everyone you would want to talk to is there, is engage in open-ended airing of thoughts, questions, and brainstorming. The only time I recall anything like that occurring was always in the form of relatively short, spontaneous "drop-in" conversations. Those were extremely valuable, but random. The conversation I had with Dawn about Kayden took maybe two minutes and only happened because I ran into her in the staff room. What really would have been revelatory would have been a meeting with Dawn, Camille, and Ed to go over what happened that day in PE when Kayden scratched me. I can only imagine the insights I could have gained from twenty minutes debriefing with those three people.

I could have emailed the three of them or used the Outlook meeting scheduler app and tried to set up a time. But the idea of doing that never occurred to me. *Why not?* The way forward lies in the many possible answers to that question. We are all on tight schedules. We have prep periods for planning. Wednesday afternoons are for team collaboration and professional development trainings. The time before students arrive and after they leave is for parent calls, emails, and more planning and set up. Another reason is that of the four of us, only two have the same job classification (Camille and I are both certificated teachers) and have the same working hours. Dawn is a classified employee and is part time. She has several job responsibilities and is not assigned to room 407 all day. Ed is not a district employee. He is a contract worker, and his time and work duties are very delineated. Finding a time for us all to meet would have been difficult. I can see us managing to meet every-once-in-a-while but certainly not on a regular basis. It very likely would require money to pay Dawn and Ed for additional time. A third reason is more intangible. Inertia? Lack of imagination? It hadn't been done before? Tracking down one coworker for a quick conversation is relatively easy. But bringing together more than two people takes planning. You have to overcome your reluctance to encroach on other people's time.

What More Can We do?

Are more meetings necessary? The answer to that question is "I hope not." Maybe we can repurpose and restructure some existing meetings. Is there really more to discuss? The answer there is definitely "yes." These are some agenda items that ought to be pursued by the stakeholders as they relate to students with special needs and PE. By stakeholders, I mean the room 407 classroom teacher, the paraeducators, the PE teacher, the physical therapist, the occupational therapist, the speech language pathologist, and behavior specialists. The agenda topics would determine which staff needed to attend a given meeting:

- Translate each student's IEP into a more functional plan/guide for PE, music, and library.
- Review students' progress.
- Review communication systems that are in use for each student, such as assistive technology.
- Discuss and evaluate teaching methods for effectiveness.
- Review unit/lesson plans for opportunities to mutually reinforce instruction.
- Training. Who needs it, and what kind?
- Adapted equipment.
- Debrief behaviors.
- Look at data: Functional Behavior Assessment (FBA), Behavior Intervention Plan (BIP), and ABC Data Sheets.
- Translate FBA and BIP into concrete plans for PE, music, and library.

It would also be valuable to have occasional contact with program directors in administration who have a macro view of special education. They tend to be absent from our world and might show up now and then to meet with the special education staff if a legal issue arises or to announce a personnel change, and then they leave. The higher up a person is in the administrative hierarchy, the less we see of them in the building. They pop in and out once in a great while. I've heard it referred to as the "dipstick" syndrome. Do administrators avoid the "trenches" because they prefer to remain in their ivory towers? Of course not! I don't believe anyone goes into special education because they are looking for an easy gig. Everyone I know sees it as their calling and loves working with students who have special needs.

Any disconnects, lapses in communication or gaps in training are most likely the result of a system that is overstressed. Resentments, frustration, and the occasional name-calling can be a by-product of that.

Teachers Are Diverse Learners and Sensory Processors Too

Think about professional development at your school or company or fishing trawler or wherever. Are people coming to the training with blank brains, preoccupied brains, or brains that are prepared for the agenda having developed some of their own thinking on the topic? I'm grateful that professional development has become so integral to our profession, and I think we can do a better job. Teachers show up to PD trainings with their heads still full of the classroom they just left, and when they gather at tables with their notebooks and coffee cups, they are prepared only to receive but not to produce. If my topic were teaching children with autism, I would like my audience to think about it beforehand, because once they are seated in the training, they will second-guess their own ideas because of perceived peer pressure, political correctness, and perhaps worries about stereotypes and bias. This is about getting people to trust their own ideas.

Another big problem with professional development when you expect people to produce some kind of creative output is the fire hose syndrome. When you pile on training after training, initiative after initiative, committee output after committee output, just please let us know what we can put off until next year. After I have processed new information from a source, whether it is a book, article, a presenter, an email from my boss, or a link to resources, I need time to reflect on it. Otherwise, it will just sink down to the bottom of my grey matter and mix with the mud. In a way, we are all just like Kayden. Load me up with too much at once, and I'm going to freak out! Welcome to the real world, you say. Adults have to multi-task, struggle through the workload, work overtime. Fine. Just adjust your expectations of work quality.

I have difficulty with an aspect of auditory processing. Scott Grafton describes it as the ability to selectively attend. It manifests when I'm listening to someone, and then there is an unrelated or contrasting sound or voice. My brain immediately drops the target voice and focuses on the interruption even when it is a background noise or conversation, and I cannot effectively balance my attention in favor of the target voice. I am unable to think or read if other people are talking around me. I am just as captivated as the next person by a good speaker, but when my mind starts to take off on a tangent that they have inspired, I'm unfortunately done listening for the moment. If a presenter gives us something to read, and people at my table start to talk, I must leave. I usually pick up my material, sit down in the hallway, and do the reading. Presenters need to pause and let their ideas sink in. Some of us need more quiet interludes to process and to let our minds zoom off into whatever mental space we need to go. If you let us do that, we will return with your ideas enriched by our own.

If I were responsible for professional development, or just for a single training on a subject, I would start with understanding my audience. In addition to the basics like how much time I had and who my audience was, I would want to know

- Their familiarity with my topic
- If I could give them an assignment ahead of time
- If there would be opportunities for follow-up

If the answer to the second item were *yes*, I would give them a writing prompt that would allow them to start thinking about my topic and formulate some of their own ideas ahead of time before they are influenced by me and by others.

Some Thoughts about Uncovering the Inventor in Each of Us

The question I posed at the beginning was: How do we create a culture of inventors? What are the most useful questions to ask? What kind of soil (pick your metaphor here) conditions do we need for this plant to grow? You will have more useful ideas per square inch if you just give free rein to your imagination, but what ignites that process, and what short circuits it? I am speaking from the perspective of a person near the end of their teaching career. I have been doing this for thirty years. What works for me will not work for you. What works for you will not work for me. When I started out, I wanted nothing more than for a mentor to hand me the formula for being a good teacher, even though I knew I probably would have to mess with it and make it my own. I can only describe the journey I've taken. The thing I know for sure is that we are each on our own journey, and that is a good thing. Think about what you like to take with you when you embark on a journey. A playlist for the car? Favorite snacks? A sketch pad? This is a playlist of sorts that I have taken with me on my teaching journey…

- Believe in yourself.
- Question all "experts."
- Don't let other people's ideas muddy the clear water of your thoughts until you've had a chance to express all that is in your mind and heart.
- Creativity is a solitary process.
- Be open to new travel partners. They come from unexpected places.
- Joining with others to come up with new ideas is not wrong – it's just in the wrong order.
- If you want your staff to be exposed to important information, do PD trainings. If you want to cultivate professional learners, choose two or three people to start the next meeting by reading a scene from Shakespeare. Or read aloud from Wilbur Wright's journals on his observations of birds in flight. Or give everyone a piece of rope and take five minutes to practice tying a bowline – one of life's most indispensable knots.

Think about It Questions

Think of a student who is not in crisis but about whom you have a vague or specific feeling of uneasiness. Perhaps it is someone who you have been meaning to pay more attention to. What are the obstacles that have prevented you from addressing the situation? If there is a gap in your knowledge about the student, who are the people who might fill it? What are the obstacles to approaching those people? Who are the people that would benefit if you were to follow through?

On page 212 there is a list of possible agenda topics for meetings with stakeholders regarding students with special needs. Create your own list. Name the people, or the job titles, who should be at that meeting.

Changing the status quo is never easy. Think of a change that you would like to make in the way your program runs that would affect other staff members and involve allocation of resources. Who are the stakeholders that would need to be your partners in the endeavor?

Epilogue

The kinds of relationships I developed with Romy, Kayden, Gemma, and Patrick would probably not be possible today. A few years ago, our school district began discontinuing specially designed PE and music classes for students with disabilities and special needs. My program endured the longest, but it too was finally terminated this year. Ironically, the straw that tipped the scale had nothing to do with dissatisfaction with the program but was staffing and budget related. Our specially designed PE program persisted as long as it did because teachers, principal, and parents believed it was in the best interest of our students.

Separate LRC II PE and music classes are an additional expense. Salaries are the biggest line item in a school district budget, and staffing numbers are based on teacher–student ratios. To have smaller classes you need to hire more teachers. In defense of our program, having the ability to move students between the Firefly PE class and gen. ed. PE allowed us to give students the program and supports that made sense for them, and that often changed throughout the year. Several of my students attended both PE classes, which was referred to by critics as "double dipping." However, that term was not used by special educators because we saw the practice as being so beneficial to students. They had the inclusion/mainstream experience, and they could receive highly individualized instruction in the smaller class when they needed it.

Instead of viewing our LRC II program as outdated and antithetical to inclusion, we saw it as the best way to give every student an appropriate PE program suited to their needs. But maintaining a specially designed class like ours opens even greater opportunities. I look at it as a foundation for "reverse mainstreaming," which is a progressive new practice in which nondisabled students take adaptive physical education classes such as wheelchair basketball. Michelle Grenier (2014) points to the growing popularity of Paralympics and disability sport teams.

> One advantage of including a disability sport curriculum within a PE program is that it can involve reverse mainstreaming whereby students without disabilities play a sport designed specifically for those with disabilities. This not only promotes sports for those with disabilities, but also levels the playing field, because students without disabilities often need to learn new skills, (such as wheelchair skills) which they do not possess.

While adaptive PE electives are available primarily at the college level, I would expect them to be adopted at the secondary level because of the obvious benefits. There are no elective classes in elementary school. However, I know from experience that if given the opportunity nondisabled and neurotypical students benefit from the experience of working with peers who have special needs. I am not just fantasizing here. The following experience confirms this.

Even as a third grader, his maturity and sensitivity caused Shawn to stand out from his classmates. Here is a typical scene: He walks up to me after entering the gym and says, "Good morning, Mr. Mokin. How's your day going?" Meanwhile all his classmates have started running around the four cones, being typical noisy third graders. "Just fine, Shawn. Thank you for asking." "You're welcome, Mr. Mokin. Okay, I'll start my warmup now. I love PE!" How could I not smile? How could I not love that kid? Maybe he wasn't sincere? Maybe it was all an act, and his parents had trained him how to please adults. But I'd known Shawn long enough and seen him in enough situations with different people to know that he was totally sincere. He was simply unique. The question I asked myself was, "Why? How did he get that way?" It took me over a year to finally learn the probable answer.

Katie came to Firefly PE when she was in kindergarten. On the spectrum, very hyperactive, prone to loud, sudden meltdowns and a frequent eloper. We made sure all the gym doors were shut when Katie was in PE. She always carried a communication iPad with her which she did not use for communication, with me but I assume that she did in her classroom. Sometimes she held it up in front of her as if she were taking videos. She spoke short phrases and referred to herself in the third person. She was independent, strong-willed, athletic, and went where she wanted to when she wanted to. Stopping her from doing that was a predictable way to set up a conflict which then often led to behavior escalation. She was too young at that point to have had a Functional Behavior Assessment, and when one was eventually written, it targeted elopement behavior and proposed a list of calm-down options.

I don't remember the context, but one day in PE Katie's behavior escalated. It went on longer, louder, and more intensely than usual. A para was trying to keep her safe and soothe her but was not having much success. She finally grabbed a radio and called down to 407. About three minutes later, to my surprise, Shawn jogged into the gym and went straight to Katie. He got down on the floor, and she immediately climbed into his lap while he hugged her and talked to her. A lightbulb went off in my head. I asked one of the EAs what Katie's last name was. It was the same as Shawn's.

A lot of things clicked into place for me that afternoon. Growing up with a younger sister like Katie must have been a partial reason for Shawn's unique maturity and sensitivity. But I guessed that it was not the complete picture. Romy, for example, also had an older brother at school. There were times when I wished he had paid more attention to his sister, but he was pretty stand-offish toward her at school. Perhaps he just needed a break from being around her at home, and school provided the freedom to be his own person and not "Romy's brother." I absolutely could not fault him. Shawn was just a unique individual. I am sure his parents had a lot to do with the way brother and sister treated each other. At that point, I started to think about the possibilities of giving our nondisabled students the experience of being peer tutors in the Firefly class.

In education, the word "inclusion" has come to be synonymous with "virtue." You can't argue with it, but it would be unfortunate if we defined it in such a way that it left no room for other options that benefit students. I believe there is a principle buried even deeper in the bedrock than inclusion. It is "Free, Appropriate Public Education."

How we as teachers, parents, program directors and coaches implement inclusive practices is what can come to be defined as "virtuous."

References

Block, M. E. (2016). *A Teacher's Guide to Adapted Physical Education*. Paul H. Brookes Publishing Co.

Couturier, L., Chepko, S., & Holt, S. A. (2014). *National Standards & Grade-Level Outcomes for K-12 Physical Education*. SHAPE America, Society of Health and Physical Educators.

Cowan, K., Malm, R. T., Lutz, A., & Murphy, C. (2013). *Five for Life Program*. Focused Fitness.

Gallwey, W.T., Kleiman, Z., Carroll, P. (1997). *The Inner Game of Tennis: The Classic Guide to the Mental Side of Peak Performance*. Random House Trade Paperbacks.

Geslak, D. S. (2015). *The Autism Fitness Handbook*. Jessica Kingsley Publishers.

Grafton, S. (2020). *Physical Intelligence: The Science of How the Body and the Mind Guide Each Other through Life*. Pantheon Books.

Grandin, T. (1995). *Thinking in Pictures: My Life with Autism*. Vintage Books.

Grenier, M. (2014). *Physical Education for Students with Autism Spectrum Disorders: A Comprehensive Approach*. Human Kinetics.

Individuals with Disabilities Act (IDEA). (n.d.). https://sites.ed.gov/idea/statuteregulations/

Koegel, L. K., & Lazebnik, C. (2004). *Overcoming Autism: Finding the Answers, Strategies, and Hope that Can Transform a Child's Life*. Penguin Books.

National Consortium for Physical Education for Individuals with Disabilities (NCPEID), Kelly, L. E. (Ed.) (2020). *Adapted Physical Education National Standards*. Human Kinetics.

Office of Special Education Programs. (2011). *Creating Equal Opportunities for Children and Youth with Disabilities to Participate in Physical Education and Extracurricular Athletics*. U.S. Department of Education Office of Special Education and Rehabilitative Services (OSERS). https://sites.ed.gov/idea/files/policy_speced_guid_idea_equal-pe.pdfz

Pangrazi, R. P. (2004). *Dynamic Physical Education for Elementary School Children*. Pearson Education, Inc.

Van Der Kolk, B. (2014). *The Body Keeps the Score: Brain, Mind, and Body in the Healing of Trauma*. Penguin Books.

Washington Education Association, Special Education Support Center. (2016). *Special Education in Washington State: A Handbook for Parents & Educators*, February 2016. http://specialeducationsupportcenter.org/resources/educators/

Index

Pages in *italics* refer to figures, pages in **bold** refer to tables, and pages followed by 'n' refer to notes.

Adapted Physical Education National Standards (APENS) 35, 108–110, 131; in lesson plans 108–110, 124, 127, 131, 159–160; motor behavior 109, 127, 131, 159, 188
adaptive goals 23, 25
Adverse Childhood Experiences (ACEs) 60
agility 53, 118, 120, 147, 165, 167, 184, 194
American Psychiatric Association 8
anchor chart 45; Counting Off 46; 4-cone track 45; Home Base 45; Relays 46; safety 52; Station Rotation 45
appropriate educational program 14, 38
appropriate learning behaviors 96
attention: focus and 191; pay attention 79–83; staying focused when distractions 83–86
attention deficit disorder (ADD) 102
atypical social communication 11
atypical social development 11
authentic learning 169
The Autism Fitness Handbook 130
autism spectrum disorder (ASD) 4, 8–13, 15, 22, 43, 75, 78, 104, 131, 164, 167, 173, 204, 206; definition 8; echolalia 9, 11, 70; prevalence 10; repetitive behaviors 8, 11; sensory disorders 79

balance and agility 120
balance balls 133, 135
ball chasing 180
ball-chasing instruction 172
ball-handling practice 168–170
ball striking 151–155
bars and play structures 135
basketballs 169, 171–172, 208
bear and crab walk 135
Behavior Intervention Plan (BIP) 66–67, 69, 173, 202, 212; desired behavior 68; replacement behavior 68; target behavior 44, 67–69, 87
behavior(s) 53, 97, 136, 204; autism 102; desired 68; discrete 192; distinct 192; elopement 66, 95, 174, 219; escalation 77, 166, 219; expected 114; functions for 67; is communication 59–60; negative 67, 88; positive 86, 88; *see also* Positive Behavior Support; problem 11; repetitive 8; replacement 68; self-stimulation 70; students' 60, 73, 89, 108, 166; target 44, 67–69, 87; triggers 61–65
biceps, triceps and quadriceps 137–138
Block, M. E. 11, 16, 30, 68–69, 86, 106, 139
body awareness and balance: APENS 108–110; physical education standards 108; SHAPE standards 108–110
body awareness and balance lesson plans: Balance Stations lesson plan 109–111; Nose to the Floor lesson plan 108–109
body composition 86, 117, 123–129, *126*

body composition and nutrition lesson plans: Calorie Burner 127–128; Food Group Laps 124–126
The Body Keeps the Score 56
bouncing 11, 52, 97, 168–169

cardiorespiratory endurance (CRE) 117, 123, 130, 133, 161–162, 184; Stomp Tag lesson plan 131–133
cardiorespiratory workout 146
Carolina Biological 137
challenge course 16, 33, 122, *123*, 162–166, *164*, 167, 173, *175*, 182, 187, 191, 193
Child Protective Services (CPS) 198
classified employee 17
classroom 44, 46, 69, 108, 210, 219; rules 88; teachers 3, 24, 41, 59, 68, 99, 116, 130, 157, 197, 199–201, 212; visual and auditory features 81
Cleanup Crew (CC) 48
climbing walls *134*, 135
close proximity/physical guidance 113
collaborating to meet challenges: being special educator 196–200, **201**; parents, students and teachers partnership 201–203; professional collaborators and topics **201**; window/iceberg? shared insights 204–205
communication 20, 23, 31, 36, 50–51, 72, 75, 85, 139, 200, 212–213, 219; behavior is 59–60, 67; clarity and total physical response 97–102; language and 4, 143, **201**; social 8, 10; verbal and nonverbal communication 8–9
compassion 20, 79
conscience/compulsion 15
cooperation opportunities 147
counselors 1–2, 6, 91, 196, **201**
cumulative mastery 92
curriculum 22, 34, 38, 114, 116–117, 121, 123, 137, 140, 164, 182, **185**, 187, 190

decision-making process 96, 138
delay-echoing speech 70
dependability 1, 91
Dewey, John 58
Diagnostic and Statistical Manual, Fifth Edition (DSM-5) 8, 10
dignity and modesty protection 70–72
direct instruction 95–97
disability sport curriculum 218
disability sport teams 218
Disney soundtracks 32
dizziness 62
double dipping 217
dribbling 63, 104, 119, 159–160, 168
duration/frequency 86–87, 191–192

educational program 12–14, 38, 66
educational services and placement 23
elementary school programs 149
elopement 65–67, 164, 166, 176, 192; behavior 66, 95, *174*, 219
English Language Learners (ELLs) 11, 21, 36–37, 101
environmental prompts *148*
equipment 4–5, 27–28, 30, 47–48, 52–53, *65*, 93, 109–110, 125, 127, 130, 132, 135, 159–161; configure *84*; different areas and pieces of 83, *92*, 95, 156, 164, 194, 197; gymnastics 173; test 121; using adaptations to access climbing wall *134*
ESL methods training 35
eye contact 104–106
"Eyes on teacher!" 96

Family Educational Rights and Privacy Act (FERPA) 24–25
Firefly(lies) 63, 65, 99, 147, 168, 177; basketball lesson 168; class/classroom 26, 112, 170; curriculum 190; lessons 207; PE class 217, 219
first two weeks of school 52

fitness activities for better health: body composition and nutrition 123–129; cardiorespiratory endurance, running, and other options 130–135; Five Health Components of Fitness 117, *117*, 140; flexibility and locomotor activities 120–123; muscle strengthening activities and physical prompts 135–139; Six-Skill-Related Fitness Components 118
fitness components 117–120, 135
fitness skills 136
flexibility 117, 120–123, 161, 193–194
Free Appropriate Public Education (FAPE) 12–14, 220
Free Choice Day 3–4
functional and socializing skills 111–113
Functional Behavior Assessment (FBA) 60, 67, 69, 202, 212, 219
functional explanation 68

Gallwey, W.T. 169–170
game skill 53, 172–173
gen. ed./general education 13, 16, 17n2, 51, 53, 217; classes/classrooms 46, 93, 137, 168, 206; curriculum 190; PE class 181
Geslak, D. S. 130
graduate teacher education program 17
Grafton, S. 79–81, 214
Grandin, T. 78
gross motor goals 25
grouping strategies: group of boys and girls 48; pair groups 48; pre-set teams 47; and team formation 54; will you be my partner? 48
gym 45–46, 49, 52, 65–66, 69, 81, 87, 93, 99, 108, 120, 169, 171, 175, 219; Engineer the Space 173–176
gymnastics: corner 173–174; setup 174–175

Handy, John 141
health-related fitness 118
healthy heart zone 120
Heart Health Stations 120
Hernandez, Patrick 32
Home Base 44, 46–47, 53, 77
human development 109, 124, 127, 131, 159
hyper/hyporeactivity 9

IEP meeting 210–212
inclusion 15, 36–41, 220
Individualized Education Programs (IEPs) 12–16, 21, 54, 60, 67, 69, 74, 88, 111, 116, 194, **201**, 201–202, 208, 212
Individuals with Disabilities Education Act (IDEA) 8, 12, 14, 201–202
The Inner Game of Tennis: The Classic Guide to the Mental Side of Peak Performance 169
instructional targets 189
intellectual disability 10, 59, 147, 209
intensity 9, 32, 38, 93, 118–120, 130, 162
Invent-a-Game Day 4
inventiveness 21
inventor mindset 19–20, 162, 166, 193
The Itsy Bitsy Spider 101

jazz 32
jump rope and challenge course 182; APENS adapted PE standards 188; health-related fitness components 184; locomotor, nonlocomotor and manipulative 187; nonlocomotor (stability) 187–188; SHAPE national standards 182–183, 187; SHAPE's critical elements for grades K-5 188; skill-related fitness components 184; SMART goals 189–190; standard 1 motor skills and movement patterns 187–188; standard 2 motor behavior 188–189; unit/lesson sequence 185, **185–187**

knowledge 58, 116, 209
Koegel, L. K. 75
K-12 Learning Standards 7–8

language and interactivity 75
language and Total Physical Response (TPR) 98–100
language, challenge 4
language, comprehension 31
language, consistency 35, 172
language development 75
language economy and specificity 102
language, generalizing across environments 107
language, sign 102
law and order 171
Lazebnik, C. 75
learning circle 53, 66, 94–97, 141, 146, 168
learning community 12
learning environment 58
learning posture 68, 87, 99, 205; lesson 102–104
learning prompt(s) 29–30, 83–86, 135–136
Learning Resource Center (LRC I) 13
Least Restrictive Environment (LRE) 14–15, 23
lesson plans 108–111, 124–128, 131–133, 159–161
life-long learning 20
locomotion 135, 142, 147, 159
locomotor activity 92, 95, 161
locomotor movement 143
locomotor patterns 119
Love and Logic 51
LRC II 13; classroom 15; program 196, 217–218

mainstreaming 16
mat circle 100–101, 148, 154, 158, 172; locomotor 143–146, *144–145*
mini tosses 97, 168
Mokin, Bill 157, 218
Monk, Thelonious 32
multi-step directions 180

muscle endurance 32, 93, 97, 117, 161, 184
muscle strengthening 135–138
music 32–34

National Child Traumatic Stress Network 56
negative behavior 67, 88
neurotypical 4, 26, 56, 113, 199, 218
non-locomotor activity 95
non-locomotor balance ball play 133
non-participation 74
nonverbal communicative behaviors 9
nonverbal communicators 190
nonverbal instruction 170

observation 83, 87, **185–186**, **201**, 204, 215
occupational therapists (OTs) 6, 23
off-task behavior 149, 175
off-task disruptive behavior 85
one-on-one instruction/one-to-one instruction 28–29, 85
on-task behavior 88
organizational system 37, 47
Our Heart Health Stations 120
outdoor play structure 111–113
Overcoming Autism (2004) 75

Pangrazi, R. P. 118
paraeducator(s) 17, 26–28, 138, 181
Paralympics 218
parent hat 195
parent–teacher meeting 202
partnering methods 48
PA system 93
pay attention 79–83, 91
pendulum 13, 154–155
personal fitness 118
personal values 20
physical assistance 135
physical conditions 78, 208
physical contact 135, 138–140
physical disabilities 15, 190
Physical Education for Students with Autism Spectrum Disorders (2014) 131

physical education (PE): academic content in 119; class 5, 16, 193; curriculum 117; environment and accommodations 26; Fireflies to 103; general 14; goal of 7; IDEA law, Sec. 300.108 14; and music classes 217; program 209, 218; regular 14; skills 150; special 14; teachers 6, 21, 24, 41–42, 44, 133; with warmup activity 46–47
physical educator 4, 108
physical environment 132
physical guidance 139
Physical Intelligence: The Science of How the Body and the Mind Guide Each Other through Life 80–81
physical learning prompts 140
physical restraint 71
physical therapists (PTs) 6, 41–42, 96, 116, 154, 191, 194, 196, **201**, 212
physical therapy 137
Picture Exchange Communication System (PECs) 68–69
play stoppages 172–173
poly spot 47, 95
positive behavior support (PBS) 69, 73, 86–88
positive reinforcement 142
power of voice 30–31
predictability 1, 61, 91
preserve a student's dignity/preserve their modesty 70
pressure seeker 78
proactive strategies for staying on task: break lesson down into pieces 179–180; create new roles 178–179; engineer the space 173–176; prerequisite game skills 172–173; reduce distance between players 176–177; use more staff/helping buddies 176–177
professional development (PD) 213
professional values 20
protective armor 131
proximity 66
public education 13, 210

public education system 17
public schools 13, 17, 138

remote teaching 5
replacement behavior 68
resistance tubes 135–137
restrictive placement 16
reverse mainstreaming 218
Revised Code of Washington (RCW) 17
routines: and scaffolds benefit diverse learners 48–52; and systems 51; warmup 46–47, 92–95

safety anchor chart 52
school psychologist 41, 196, **201**
self-contained special education classroom 208
self-harm 67
self-monitoring 85
self-stimulation behavior 70
sense of sensory input 81
sensory break 68
sensory break menu 73, 77
sensory diversity 76–79
sensory environment 77–79, 82–83
shakable noise-makers 34
Shakespeare 215
SHAPE America National Standards 108–110, 182
SHAPE's National K-12 Standards 7, 131
skill-related fitness 118
sleepaway camp experience 91
social communication 8, 10
social/communicative impairments 106
social-emotional content 58
social/emotional goals 25
social-emotional reciprocity 8, 11
social interaction 8–9, 98
social norms 139
solo exercise 146
special education 12–13, 16–17, 212; definition 12; program failure 210; services 17; students/special ed. students/SPED students 12–13; teachers 6, 197, 199, 206
Special Education Team 200

special educators 139, 217
specific gross motor objectives 25
Specific, Measurable, Achievable, Realistic, and Time (SMART) goals 189–190
specific objectives 25
speech language pathologist (SLP) 6, 23, 49–50, 197–198
Sport Pack 106
sports and chasing/fleeing games 130
squeeze space 102
stack cups 106–107
station rotations 4, 32, 38, 40, 53–54, 84, 110, 114, 121, 153, **185**
Student Incident Reflection Tool 65, 89
students': academic content 85; adapted equipment 194; assessment & measuring growth with 190–193; attention and engagement 81; with autism 113; behavior triggers 89; communication deficits 85; dignity 70–72, 74, 139; with disabilities 12, 56, 59, 73, 205, 217; disability/difference 177; ELL 199–200; emotional state 59; expectations 97; as having special needs/with special needs 13; health condition 74; kindergarten 119; maintaining student engagement 74–76; managing class when student escalates 72–74; minority groups of 15; movements and vocalizations 69–70; my class of students with special needs 15; as my special education students 15; preferences and preferred activities 87; public school 201; sensory diversity 76–79; sensory idiosyncrasies 79; with special needs 203, 207, 210, 217; unregulated behavior 71, 73
successes and failures 209–211
Summer Samba 32
systems/routines 44

target behavior 44, 87
targeted elopement behavior 219

teachers: certificated 17; diverse learners and sensory processors 213–214; ELL 34; ESL 143; PD trainings 213; of record 41–42; special education 197, 199, 206
teacher–student relationship 57, 59
technology 98, 139
thumps 119
tossing 173; and catching 168–169; rolling/skipping 104
total physical response (TPR) 97–102, 158
track lesson plans: Double Track lesson plan 159–160; Inside Track/Outside Track lesson plan 160–161
track, mobile learning platform 52–53
trial-error-modification 116, 162, 207, 209
trustworthy 140
tumbling 135

unregulated behavior 72–73

Van Der Kolk, B. 56
Velcro schedule poster 149
verbal and nonverbal communication 8–9
verbal instructions 169
verbal/nonverbal behavior 9, 11
virtue 179, 220
visual/hands-on learning 102
visual schedule 48–50, *50*, 54
visual vocabulary chart 99
vocalizations 69–70

warmup 92–95; activity 46–47; laps 94–95, 168; routines 47, 114; track 92–95
Washington Administrative Code (WAC) 12
Washington Post 198
Washington State law 17
weighted blanket 68
well-designed lesson 88
wheels 149–150, *151*
whole-class discussion 35
Wright, Wilbur 215

For Product Safety Concerns and Information please contact our EU
representative GPSR@taylorandfrancis.com
Taylor & Francis Verlag GmbH, Kaufingerstraße 24, 80331 München, Germany

www.ingramcontent.com/pod-product-compliance
Lightning Source LLC
Chambersburg PA
CBHW050630300426
44112CB00012B/1741